W9-BLF-205

FOCUS GROUPS
3rd Edition
A PRACTICAL GUIDE FOR APPLIED RESEARCH

RICHARD A. KRUEGER & MARY ANNE CASEY

Sage Publications, Inc.
International Educational and Professional Publisher
Thousand Oaks ▪ London ▪ New Delhi

Cartoons by Dale Mann; copyright © 2000 by Richard Krueger and Mary Anne Casey.

For information:

Sage Publications, Inc.
2455 Teller Road
Thousand Oaks, California 91320
E-mail: order@sagepub.com

Sage Publications Ltd.
6 Bonhill Street
London EC2A 4PU
United Kingdom

Sage Publications India Pvt. Ltd.
M-32 Market
Greater Kailash I
New Delhi 110 048 India

Printed in the United States of America

Library of Congress Cataloging-in-Publication Data

Krueger, Richard A.
   Focus groups: A practical guide for applied research / by
Robert A. Krueger, Mary Anne Casey—3rd ed.
       p.   cm.
Includes bibliographical references and index.
   ISBN 0-7619-2070-6 (cloth: acid-free paper)
   ISBN 0-7619-2071-4 (pbk.: acid-free paper)
   1. Focused group interviewing.   2. Social sciences—Methodology.
I. Casey, Mary Anne. II. Title.
   H61.28.K78   2000
   381.6'1'068—dc21   00-008040

00 01 02 03 10 9 8 7 6 5 4 3 2 1

Acquiring Editor:	C. Deborah Laughton
Editorial Assistant:	Eileen Carr
Production Editor:	Diana E. Axelsen
Editorial Assistant:	Victoria Cheng
Typesetter/Designer:	Janelle LeMaster
Indexer:	Mary Mortensen
Cover Designer:	Ravi Balasuriya

Contents

Preface

We want people to listen to us. We want our partners, our kids, our colleagues, our bosses, our politicians, and the clerk at the store to listen to us. We want them to pay attention, to show they are listening, and to be open to what we have to say. Why does it so often feel like we aren't being heard? People are busy. They listen selectively. People catch fragments of what was said. They tune out things they don't want to hear. In Western society, we talk too quickly, we interrupt too often, and we feel we must respond.

Focus group interviewing is about listening. It is about paying attention. It is about being open to hear what people have to say. It is about being nonjudgmental. It is about creating a comfortable environment for people to share. It is about being careful and systematic with the things people tell you. When used appropriately, the process improves listening, and the results can be used to benefit the people who shared the information. And people go away feeling good about having been heard.

How Is This Edition Different?

We've tried to make this edition more fun to look at and read. The oversized pages, touch of color, and extra white space make the pages more appealing. We also added illustrations designed to make you smile.

The book is still full of advice based on years of experience conducting focus groups. It is designed as a guide and a reference book for those who are conducting focus groups, contracting for focus groups, or teaching about focus groups. We've included examples. We've outlined processes.

When compared to the first and second editions, this third edition has even more "how-to." There is an expanded description of how we plan focus group studies, examples of questions that ask participants to do more than just discuss, and suggestions on how to answer questions about your focus group research. There is also more on analysis. Faculty members have told us they wanted help teaching graduate students how to analyze focus group data. This can be an overwhelming, lonely, and frustrating part of doing focus groups. Our challenge was to make the process less nebulous. We have tried to outline the types of decisions we make when doing analysis in a step-by-step process. It is a more concrete description of analysis than in earlier editions.

There is also a new chapter that compares and contrasts four different approaches to focus group research: the market research approach, the academic approach, the nonprofit approach, and the participatory approach. The traditions, purposes, accepted practices, and expected outcomes of these approaches vary, but we haven't seen any writings that describe these differences. The chapter presents a range of ways focus groups are conducted.

Here is how the book is organized: Chapter 1 is intended to set the stage for focus group research. This section describes the history of focus groups and identify those essential elements that are needed to truly call it a focus group. Chapters 2 through 7 contain the best practices for conducting focus group research. Quality focus groups demand effective planning (Chapter 2), good questions (Chapter 3), skillful moderating (Chapter 4), selecting the right participants (Chapter 5), systematic analysis (Chapter 6), and appropriate reporting (Chapter 7). We've tried to suggest practical strategies for achieving good practice. The final chapters concentrate less on how-to strategies and more on special concerns and adaptations. Focus group research continues to evolve, and in Chapter 8, we suggest features and characteristics of four distinct paths. Chapter 9 gives an overview of how focus groups are being adapted to special audiences, and then in Chapter 10, we identify emerging uses of focus group research. In the final chapter (Chapter 11), we offer suggestions on how to answer questions about focus group research.

This book is particularly intended for aspiring researchers, so we give a lot of advice about how to do things—like we would suggest to a friend, a graduate student, or a client. But when talking to a friend or a client, we modify our advice to fit their situation. We can't be that specific in this book. So think about how our advice fits your audience and environment. The age, culture, lifestyle, or occupation of your participants may mean you have to modify the practices. For example, having precise beginning and ending times may be important in a corporate culture but be inappropriate in certain community settings. We don't mean for our advice to be rigid. Instead, use it as a way to get started, think about how it needs to be adapted, and get advice from wise ones.

What Have We Learned?

Sure, we learned about the process. These are the kinds of things we share in this book. We learned to plan, to recruit, to moderate, and to analyze. And we keep learning new things about the process. That is the head stuff. It is important because it allows us to learn the more important stuff. The stuff that changes us as people. The heart and gut stuff.

Through focus groups, we have gotten tiny glimpses of worlds that we otherwise do not experience. What it is like to suffer from psychosis. What it is like to live with someone who has severe and chronic depression. What it is like to be a veteran. What it is like to be a new mom. What it is like to be a parent of a child who attends special education classes. What it is like to be beaten and degraded by someone you love. What it is like to be a second-grade boy. Why farmers feel they are unjustly blamed for environmental issues. How young Black urban men view guns. How environmentalists are torn between publicizing treasured resources so people can enjoy them and keeping them a secret so they won't be destroyed. How the views of frontline health care providers differ from views of management. What it is like for Hmong parents who have to rely on their children to read letters from school because the parents can't read English.

Some of the stories we have heard have been funny, some have been uplifting, and some have haunted us for years. These stories have changed us. We have learned that there are always multiple realities. Depending on where a person is in the world, he or she sees things differently. By carefully listening, we get an image of how they think and feel and why. Because of this, we hope we've learned to be less judgmental. We hope we've learned more about how to treat people with respect. We hope we've learned to hear the wisdom that people share. We hope we've learned to be trustworthy messengers. We know we have learned that it is an honor to sit with people and hear their stories.

About the Icons

Throughout this volume, icons are used to identify materials of interest. These icons serve several purposes:

The **BACKGROUND** icon identifies the bigger picture and places the current discussion into a broader context.

The **TIP** icon highlights a good practice to follow or something that has worked successfully for us.

The **EXAMPLE** icon highlights stories and illustrations of general principles.

The **CAUTION** icon indicates an area where you should be careful. These are especially intended to help beginners spot potholes or potential roadblocks.

The **CHECKLIST** icon identifies a list of items that are good to think about.

Acknowledgments

For the record, we want to applaud the work of public employees. There is a perception that government workers don't work hard. It certainly isn't true for the ones we've met. They have been committed, passionate, hardworking people trying to make the world a better place. They are good people who care. They want to listen. They work hard to do the right thing.

Here are some of the people we have been lucky to work with. They gave us opportunities to learn about, practice, and teach the art and science of listening through focus groups. Our thanks to them.

Carol Bryant with the School of Public Health, University of South Florida and James Lindenberger with Best Start Social Marketing in Florida

Bob Djupstrom and Susan Balgie with the Minnesota Department of Natural Resources

Bonnie Bray, Joel Hetler, and Linda Hall with the Ramsey County Children's Mental Health Collaborative

Gretchen Taylor, Junie Svenson, and Betty Kaplan with the Minnesota Department of Health

Nancy Wilson, Carter Mecher, Carol Craft, and Bunny Huller along with Ann Strong and her team of focus group moderators with the U.S. Department of Veterans Affairs

Jon Morris, Barbara McIntyre, and Carmen Medina with the U.S. government

Gail Redd from the Office of Personnel Management

Ed Nelson with the Wisconsin Department of Natural Resources

Jose Calderon and his colleagues at Drew University of Medicine and Science

Maryann Cunningham and her talented staff from the University of Tennessee

JoAnn Muniz with the Environmental Protection Agency in Boston

Harold Cook with Cook Research

Marilyn Rausch, gifted professional moderator

David Morgan from Portland State University

Chuck Casey, Jean King, Cynthia McArthur, Dianne Neumark-Steiner, and Mary Story of the University of Minnesota

Mike Patton, evaluator extraordinaire, author, explorer, teller of tales

Rosalind Hurworth with the University of Melbourne

Penny Hawkins with the government of New Zealand

Karl Murray of NASDSE

The good sports of the Phillips Lead Project

Also a big thank you to Dale Mann, the cartoonist whose work enlivens this book. And thanks to C. Deborah Laughton of Sage Publications for escorting this third edition through the publishing process.

We have more information now than we can use, and less knowledge and understanding than we need. Indeed, we seem to collect information because we have the ability to do so, but we are so busy collecting it that we haven't devised means of using it. The true measure of any society is not what it knows but what it does with what it knows.

—Warren Bennis

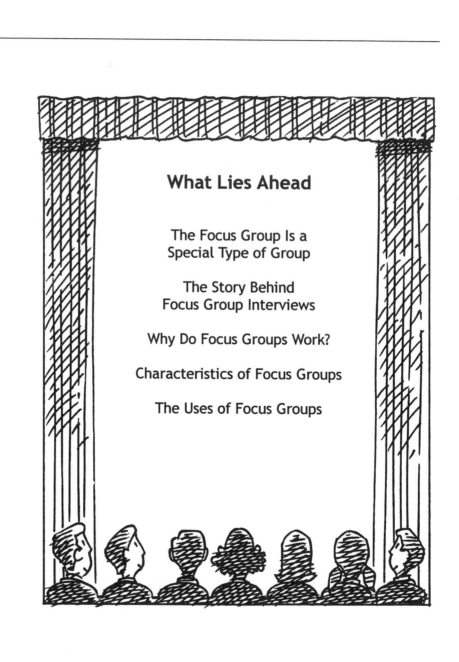

What Lies Ahead

The Focus Group Is a
Special Type of Group

The Story Behind
Focus Group Interviews

Why Do Focus Groups Work?

Characteristics of Focus Groups

The Uses of Focus Groups

1

Overview of Focus Groups

Groups are a common experience. We find ourselves invited, herded, or seduced into groups for planning, decision making, advising, brainstorming, learning, sharing, and self-help. Groups can be fun and fruitful, but they can also be agonizing experiences that are unnecessary, unproductive, and time-consuming. We believe there are two reasons group experiences turn into wasted time. The leaders are fuzzy about the purpose and/or the process.

Sometimes, the purpose of the group is clearly understood, such as when a nominating committee convenes to develop a slate of officer candidates. At other times, the purpose of the group is vague or perceived differently by different participants. The function of the group may be to suggest ideas, to clarify potential options, to react to ideas, to recommend a course of action, to make a decision, to plan, or to evaluate. Each purpose is different from the others. If leaders aren't clear about the purpose of the group, or if they say it is one thing but lead the group in another direction, participants get confused and frustrated.

Even if the leader is clear about the purpose, he or she may not have the skills needed to guide the group. Group process skills are essential if the group is to accomplish its purpose. But the skills necessary for leading one type of group experience may not work in another. The processes used to get participants' reactions to ideas are different from the processes used for group decision making.

The purpose of this book is to help you—the reader—to learn to do focus group research. We will share what we have learned—what has worked for us. We hope that you will be clearer about the purpose of focus groups and the processes used to conduct focus group research.

The Focus Group Is a Special Type of Group

A focus group isn't just getting a bunch of people together to talk. A focus group is a special type of group in terms of purpose, size, composition, and procedures. The purpose of a focus group is to listen and gather information. It is a way to better understand how people feel or think about an issue, product, or service. Participants are selected because they have certain characteristics in common that relate to the topic of the focus group.

The researcher creates a permissive environment in the focus group that encourages participants to share perceptions and points of view, without pressuring participants to vote or reach consensus. And you don't do just one focus group. The group discussion is conducted several times with similar types of participants so the researcher can identify trends and patterns. Then careful and systematic analysis of the discussions provides clues and insights as to how a product, service, or opportunity is perceived.

PURPOSE: To understand how people feel or think about an issue, product, service or idea.

Six to eight PEOPLE selected because they have something in common.

Skilled MODERATOR

Comfortable, permissive ENVIRONMENT

A focus group study is a carefully planned series of discussions designed to obtain perceptions on a defined area of interest in a permissive, nonthreatening environment. Each group is conducted with six to eight people by a skilled interviewer. The discussions are relaxed, and often participants enjoy sharing their ideas and perceptions. Group members influence each other by responding to ideas and comments of others.

The Story Behind
Focus Group Interviews

Focus groups have become popular. Over the past three decades, the label *focus groups* has been applied to many different group encounters—indeed, some require a stretch of imagination to be called focus groups! We have heard town meetings, reading groups, and study circles being called focus groups. Recently, more than 300 people gathered in a school auditorium for what was called a "focus group." We know it wasn't a focus group because it didn't contain the essential elements of focus group interviewing. These essential elements grew out of early work with focus group interviewing.

In the late 1930s, social scientists began investigating alternative ways of conducting interviews. Some social scientists had doubts about the accuracy of traditional individual interviews that used a predetermined questionnaire with closed-ended response choices. This approach had a major disadvantage: The respondent was limited by the choices offered, and therefore the findings could be unintentionally influenced by the interviewer through oversight or omission. Stuart A. Rice was one of the first social scientists to express concern. In 1931, he wrote,

> A defect of the interview for the purposes of factfinding in scientific research, then, is that the questioner takes the lead. That is, the subject plays a more or less passive role. Information or points of view of the highest value may not be disclosed because the direction given the interview by the questioner leads away from them. In short, data obtained from an interview are as likely to embody the preconceived ideas of the interviewer as the attitudes of the subject interviewed. (Rice, 1931, p. 561)

Social scientists began exploring strategies whereby the researcher would take on a less directive and dominating role. Respondents would be able to comment on the areas they thought were most important. Nondirective interviewing shifted attention from the interviewer to the respondent, placing emphasis on getting in tune with the reality of the interviewee. Nondirective interviews used open-ended questions and allowed individuals to respond without setting boundaries or providing clues for potential response categories. The open-ended approach allowed the subject ample opportunity to comment, explain, and share experiences and attitudes. Nondirective interviewing increased in appeal in the late 1930s and 1940s. Roethlisberger and Dickson (1938) cited it in studies of employee motivation and Carl Rogers (1942) in psychotherapy.

During World War II, social scientists began using the nondirective interviewing technique in groups—the beginning of focus groups. In one of the first focus group studies, Robert Merton explored morale in the U.S. military for the War Department. He found that people revealed sensitive information when they felt they were in a safe, comfortable place with people like themselves. Many of the procedures that have come to be accepted as common practice in focus group interviews were set forth in the classic work by Robert K. Merton, Marjorie Fiske, and Patricia L. Kendall, *The Focused Interview* (1956).

Although Merton is and was a giant in sociology, most academics did not embrace the focused interview. In fact, Merton's pioneering work laid dormant in the social sciences for decades. The acceptance of focus groups and of qualitative research methods in general was delayed in academic circles for a variety of reasons—a preoccupation with quantitative procedures, assumptions about the nature of reality, and a societal tendency to believe in numbers. Social science research paid attention to experimental designs, control groups, and randomization. This sojourn with numbers has been beneficial because we gained in our experimental sophistication, but it also nurtured a desire for more understanding of the human experience. Too often, the quantitative approaches were based on imperfect assumptions about people, things, or reality in general.

Even though academics weren't interested in focus groups, the pragmatic market research community embraced focus groups beginning in the 1950s. Business was booming after the war, and market researchers were charged with finding out how to make their company's product most attractive to potential customers.

Focus group interviews are widely accepted within marketing research because they produce believable results at a reasonable cost. Business owners know the importance of creating a desirable product, advertising that product, and introducing that product to the public.

The sensible strategy is to stay in touch with customers. Products have undergone major revisions in design, packaging, or advertising due to findings in focus groups. Advertising campaigns often focus on what the consumer considers to be the positive attributes of the product. For example, soft drink companies discovered via focus groups that consumers often drink beverages because of the sociability features associated with the product, not because they are thirsty. It is no wonder that slogans promoting these beverages highlight how "things go better" or increase personal popularity on the beach (Bellenger, Bernhardt, & Goldstrucker, 1976).

Since the 1950s, the use of focus groups in the for-profit sector has grown so much that a whole industry has been created to support focus group research. In every major city across the United States, market research firms provide services relating to focus groups: finding the right participants, recruiting them, catering for groups, rooms with one-way mirrors, and video- and audiotaping options. In every major city, there are also professional focus group moderators who spend their lives conducting focus groups for businesses. The technique had evolved since Merton's time from a social science research method to a method designed to serve businesses well.

In the 1980s, academics began rediscovering focus group interviewing, often learning from market researchers. But some of the accepted practices in business focus groups just didn't work well in academic or nonprofit settings. Academics took some of the practical strategies from market researchers and adapted the technique to work with other audiences. These scholars also returned to the work of Merton to learn how the technique was originally used.

Several distinct approaches to focus group interviewing have evolved since Merton began his work. One approach emerges out of the consumer-oriented market research tradition. Another emerges from the academic and scientific environment. A third approach is found in the nonprofit and public environment. Yet a fourth comes from the participatory research environment where community members or volunteers are involved as researchers in the study. Each approach is distinctive but has the common elements of focus group research. These different approaches are discussed in greater length in Chapter 8.

Why Do Focus Groups Work?

The intent of the focus group is to promote self-disclosure among participants. We want to know what people really think and feel. For some individuals, self-disclosure comes easily—it is natural and comfortable. But for others, it is difficult or uncomfortable and requires trust, effort, and courage. Or disclosure may be easy in some settings but not others. Children have a natural tendency to disclose things about themselves, but through socialization they learn the value of dissemblance. Over time, the natural and spontaneous disclosures of children are modified by social pressure. Sidney Jourard expands on this tendency:

> As children we are, and we act, our real selves. We say what we think, we scream for what we want, we tell what we did. These spontaneous disclosures meet variable consequences—some disclosures are ignored, some rewarded, and some punished. Doubtless in accordance with the laws of reinforcement, we learn early to withhold certain disclosures because of the painful consequences to which they lead. We are punished in our society, not only for what we actually do, but also for what we think, feel, or want. Very soon, then, the growing child learns to display a highly expurgated version of his self to others. I have coined the term "public self" to refer to the concept of oneself which one wants others to believe. (Jourard, 1964, p. 10)

A familiar story, especially for mothers, is that of a child running home to tell of an exciting and possibly dangerous experience. Mom is horrified at the tale and tells the child to never, never do that again. Mom's unexpected response leaves an indelible impression, and the child learns one of two things: Either never repeat the experience or, if you do, don't tell Mom!

A young mother was visiting the Sunday school class of her 6-year-old daughter. The lesson was on proper behavior in church. The teacher asked the children to name places where we should not run. Lots of hands were raised, and the teacher called on one child at a time. The children offered their answers: school, the library, grocery store—but church was not mentioned. The visiting mother proudly noticed that her daughter's hand was still waving in the air, undoubtedly armed with the answer sought by the teacher. Finally the teacher called on the daughter. With great enthusiasm, the 6-year-old responded, "The liquor store—my dad said that I should never run in the liquor store because I'll knock down the bottles." The mother was momentarily spellbound because liquor stores were held in disrepute by this church. The child had not yet developed a "public self" at least as far as the church was concerned.

So when do people self-disclose? When do they say what they really think and feel? It is when they feel comfortable and when the environment is permissive and nonjudgmental. Think about bus, train, or plane rides. People are seated close to strangers for hours. It is not unusual for travelers to strike up a casual conversation in which they share information about themselves. In some circumstances, the travelers begin to reveal personal attitudes and feelings about work, family, or life that they might not share with acquaintances. This self-disclosure occurs for several reasons: One or both of the travelers may have sensed that they were alike, the environment is nonthreatening, and even if one disapproved of what was heard, the travelers will likely never see each other again. Linda Austin, a psychiatrist at the Medical University of South Carolina, was interviewed by Julie Schmit in *USA Today*: "If you reveal something about yourself to a stranger, so what? There are no consequences. Once you get off the plane, the relationship, which can become very deep very quick, is over" (Schmit, 1993, pp. 1B-2B).

Another reason travelers readily disclose is that they perceive they are alike in some way. It may be that they have one or more characteristics in common, such as age, gender, occupation, or marital status, or that they hold similar attitudes on a topic of discussion. Jourard (1964) has found that individuals decide to reveal based on their perceptions of the other person. In his studies of self-disclosure, Jourard found that "subjects tended to disclose more about themselves to people who resembled them in various ways than to people who differ from them" (p. 15).

Our goal is to create a comfortable, permissive environment in focus groups. We always select participants who have something in common, and we tell them they have this thing in common. The moderator is not in a position of power or influence and encourages comments of all types—positive and negative. The interviewer is careful not to make judgments about the responses and to control body language that might communicate approval or disapproval. The role of the moderator is to ask questions, listen, keep the conversation on track, and make sure everyone has a chance to share. The groups are held in locations where the participants will be comfortable. This will be different for teens than for corporate employees. It may be someone's home, the church basement, a pizza joint, a community center, a neighborhood coffee shop, or a business conference room. Often, when talking to participants, we call it a small group discussion, rather than a focus group, so the process doesn't seem intimidating or mysterious. We try to make people feel comfortable.

Characteristics of Focus Groups

Focus group interviews typically have five characteristics or features. These characteristics relate to the ingredients of a focus group: (1) people who (2) possess certain characteristics and (3) provide qualitative data (4) in a focused discussion (5) to help understand the topic of interest. Other types of group processes used in human services (delphic, brainstorming, nominal, planning, therapeutic, advisory, etc.) may also have one or more of these features but not in the same combination as focus group interviews.

Focus Groups Involve People

Focus groups are typically composed of five to ten people, but the size can range from as few as four to as many as twelve. The group must be small enough for everyone to have an opportunity to share insights and yet large enough to provide diversity of perceptions. When the group exceeds a dozen participants, there is a tendency for the group to fragment. Participants want to talk but are unable to do so because there is just not a sufficient pause in the conversation. In these situations, participants share by whispering to the people next to them. This is a signal that the group is too big. Small groups of four or five participants afford more opportunity to share ideas, but the restricted size also results in a smaller pool of total ideas. These smaller groups— sometimes called *mini-focus groups*—have a distinct advantage in logistics. Groups of four or five can be easily accommodated in restaurants, homes, and other environments where space is at a premium.

The People Possess Certain Characteristics

Focus groups are composed of participants who are similar to each other in a way that is important to the researcher. The nature of this homogeneity is determined by the purpose of the study. This similarity is a basis for recruitment, and participants are typically informed of these common factors at the beginning of the discussion.

This homogeneity can be broadly or narrowly defined. For example, suppose an adult community education program wanted to know more about how to reach people who haven't participated in their programs. In this case, homogeneity could be broadly defined as adults who live in the community who have not yet attended community education sessions. Group members could vary by age, gender, occupation, and interests, but members have the commonality of being adults, community members, and nonusers. If, however, the community education staff are interested in attracting more parents of children younger than age 5, residents in specific neighborhoods, or people who work at home, then the researcher would use a narrower definition of homogeneity in selecting participants. The issue is, Who can give you the type of information you need?

Focus groups have traditionally been composed of people who do not know each other. For years it was considered ideal if participants were complete strangers. More recently, however, researchers are questioning the necessity and practicality of this guideline, especially in community-based studies. In some communities, it is virtually impossible to locate strangers. Caution should still be used when considering focus groups with close friends, family members or relatives, or closely knit work groups. Grouping people who regularly interact, either socially or at work, may inhibit disclosure on certain topics.

The moderator also has certain characteristics that can inhibit or support group sharing. If the moderator is readily identified with the organization or, for that matter, identified with any controversial issue in the community, the quality of the results could be jeopardized. For example, the top administrator of a statewide nonprofit institution was convinced that focus groups would provide valuable insights into the concerns of field staff. The administrator wanted to moderate these discussions with subordinates. Not a good idea. He was clearly in a power position. He made final decisions on salary, job responsibilities, and hiring and firing. We encouraged the administrator to find a neutral moderator outside the organizational chain of command.

Focus Groups Provide Qualitative Data

The goal of a focus group is to collect data that are of interest to the researcher—typically to find the range of opinions of people across several groups. The researcher compares and contrasts data collected from at least three focus groups. This differs from other group interactions in which the goal is to come to some conclusion at the end of a discussion—reach consensus, provide recommendations, or make decisions among alternatives. The focus group presents a more natural environment than that of an individual interview because participants are influencing and influenced by others—just as they are in life. The researcher serves several functions in the focus group: moderator, listener, observer, and eventually analyst using an inductive process.

The inductive researcher derives understanding based on the discussion as opposed to testing a preconceived hypothesis or theory.

Focus Groups Have a Focused Discussion

The questions in a focus group are carefully predetermined. The questions are phrased and sequenced so they are easy to understand and logical to the participant. Most are open-ended questions. These questions appear spontaneous but are developed through considerable reflection and input. The set of questions—called the questioning route or interview guide—is then arranged in a natural, logical sequence. Questions near the beginning of the group are more general. As the group continues, the questions become more specific—more focused. The beginning questions help get people talking and thinking about the topic. Questions near the end of the group typically yield the most useful information. There is no pressure by the moderator to have the group reach consensus. Instead, attention is placed on understanding the feelings, comments, and thought processes of participants as they discuss the issues.

The Uses of Focus Groups

Focus groups work particularly well to determine the perceptions, feelings, and thinking of people about issues, products, services, or opportunities. Here are some of the ways the information gathered in focus groups is used. These categories are not intended to be mutually exclusive or all-inclusive. Instead, they present a beginning way to think of the variety of uses of focus group interviewing.

Decision Making

Earlier we said that focus groups aren't used for decision making. Now we're saying they are. Here is the difference—when using focus groups, decisions are made after all the focus groups are completed, not in individual groups. Also, the decisions are made by designated decision makers using the findings from the focus groups, not by focus group participants. The focus groups are used to gain understanding about a topic so decision makers can make more informed choices.

Focus group findings have been used to advise decision making before, during, or after an event or program. When focus groups are used to gather information before a program, we call it needs assessment, asset analysis, a climate survey, planning, pilot testing, and so on. When focus groups are used during a program, we call it formative evaluation, process evaluation, feedback, monitoring, reporting, and so on. When they are used for decision making after an event, it might be called summative evaluation, outcome evaluation, or just feedback.

Product or Program Development

A slightly different way of thinking about focus group information is to consider the stages in product or program development. This model grows out of the commercial business and industry environment, but we have been cheerleaders for the idea in the nonprofit and public sector. We've illustrated the wrong way to plan in Illustration 1.1 and a better way to plan in Illustration 1.2.

Illustration 1.1. The Wrong Way to Plan

Illustration 1.2. A Better Way to Plan

There are three points in the development of a product or program when focus groups are helpful. The first, which is early in the development, is used to gain understanding—to see the issue through the eyes and hearts of the target audience. The goal of these focus groups is to learn how a target audience sees, understands, and values a particular topic and to learn the language used to talk about the topic. How do they think about it? How do they feel about it? How do they talk about it? What do they like about it? What do they dislike about it? What would get them to use the service or product or start or stop a behavior? What keeps them from doing it (breast-feeding), using it (your program), or buying it? Design experts then use these findings to create prototypes for the program or product. They develop several different designs of varying cost, intensity, duration, and so on based on what was learned from the first-phase focus groups.

The second series of focus groups pilot tests the prototypes the design experts came up with. Potential users are asked to compare and contrast each option. They are asked what they like and what they don't like.

The designers are then asked to take what they learned from the pilot test focus groups and design one best product or program design. If the redesign is major and there are substantial financial risks, additional focus groups might be used to test the final design before it is produced or implemented.

Focus groups can also be helpful after a product is on the market or a program is up and running. They can be used for evaluation. How can the product or program be improved? Does it achieve the expected results? What works well and what doesn't?

This three-stage process of focus group research was first used in the development of consumer products, but it has been helpful in many other areas as well. These stages have been beneficial in developing advertising campaigns, curriculum materials, logos, and social marketing efforts.

Customer Satisfaction

Focus groups are often used early in a customer satisfaction study to define the concept of satisfaction, identify the relevant ingredients of satisfaction, and discover the conditions or circumstances that influence satisfaction. Armed with this information, survey researchers can then design instruments that can quantify satisfaction by region, type of use, customer demographics, or other relevant variables. Designing the quantifiable instrument before listening to consumers has been found to be hazardous to organizational health and well-being.

Planning and Goal Setting

Some public institutions use focus groups to help them plan and set goals. They purposefully and systematically listen to clients and employees to learn how they see the organization and where it should head. What are its strengths? Weaknesses? What's missing? What opportunities exist? What are the advantages and disadvantages of moving in this particular direction?

Over time, organizations tend to institutionalize, streamline, or abridge planning processes, often with the best intentions. Unfortunately, these changes begin to fracture the relationship between the client and the organization. The client begins to feel that the organization is not responsive to his or her unique needs because the evidence used for planning by the organization is not visible and sometimes not understood or valued by the client. Ironically, the organization may be using sophisticated procedures for discerning public needs, but the individual perceives it as ineffective because there are no obvious indications that the organization is listening. In this environment, focus groups have two advantages. Focus groups not only yield valuable insights from customers and clients, but also convey that the organization wants to listen. There is a substantial difference to the individual between the organizational listening that occurs within a focus group and that which occurs in a public hearing or meeting.

Another way that organizations are using focus groups for planning is in identifying different scenarios that could result from policies, programs, future events, disasters, and so on. Focus groups composed of experts, often from differing backgrounds or disciplines, are asked to reflect on the aftereffects of these situations. Listening to others with differing expertise and allowing focus group participants an opportunity to interact can foster new insights and solutions not available by traditional strategies.

Needs Assessment

Arguably, one of the most difficult tasks facing a nonprofit or public organization is that of needs assessment. What seems so simple on the surface—a discovery of needs—is often remarkably complex. Focus groups have proven helpful mostly because they provide an interactive environment. Focus groups enable people to ponder, reflect, and listen to experiences and opinions of others. This interaction helps participants compare their own personal reality to that of others.

Needs are tricky because sometimes the need the sponsor wants to explore is only part of the problem. This is often the case when conducting employee needs assessments for training. An employer thinks, "We should train our people so they do more of X or less of X or do X better." But in focus groups, what begins as a listing of training needs quickly evolves into a discussion of what it would really take to get them to do more X or be better at X—changes in procedures, rewards and motivation, communications, and organizational culture. To organizational leaders, training and related education experiences are often seen as solutions, whereas the participants of focus groups regularly see a disconnection between the problem and the solution. Employers want to "fix" the people. The employees point to problems with the system. Training is one way of changing employee behavior, but employees are often frustrated by organizational barriers or a lack of incentives that thwart change.

Quality Movements

Focus groups have been helpful in developing and maintaining quality improvement efforts. These quality efforts depend on widespread involvement, open communications, feedback, and a nonthreatening environment. Focus groups are one of the strategies used to define quality, test monitoring procedures or solution ideas, and generally understand issues relating to quality.

Understanding Employee Concerns

Public and nonprofit organizations have many of the same types of employee concerns as other organizations. There are concerns about employee morale and motivation, incentives and barriers to productivity, influence of merit pay and compensation procedures, concern about how welcoming the environment is to different kinds of diversity, and a host of other topics relating to human resource development. Focus groups with employees have been helpful in understanding the perspectives of staff and also in identifying or testing potential policies or solution strategies.

Policy Making and Testing

In the past decade, a number of public organizations have used focus groups to help develop and test policy strategies prior to implementation. Focus groups have been helpful in identifying and understanding the criteria needed for successful rules, laws, or policies. Then, by using focus groups to pilot test the policies or procedures, the public organization can determine which options are easiest for the public to adopt or follow, easiest to understand, and easiest for the agency to enforce.

A Primary or Secondary Research Tool

Focus groups are used as a research procedure. Research, however, can be seen in a variety of ways with differing end results. For example, *academic research* is often conducted by students and faculty at institutions of higher education and seeks to provide insights that are shared through journals, papers, and books. By contrast, *social marketing research* is more similar to its cousin, marketing research, on the surface; it seeks to provide strategies for changing behavior in a socially desirable manner. Still another type—*evaluation research*—is aimed at helping program decision makers and answering public questions of accountability and worth of programs. Still another variation is *participatory research,* which places emphasis on involving people in a community in conducting the research, because of what the process does for that community in terms of developing commitment, capacity, and talents as well as improving utilization.

SUMMARY

Focus groups are special creatures in the kingdom of groups. In terms of appearances, focus groups look very much like other kinds of group experiences. On closer inspection, however, focus groups have a distinctive cluster of characteristics:

1. Focus groups involve homogeneous people in a social interaction.
2. The purpose of focus groups is to collect qualitative data from a focused discussion.
3. Focus group interviewing is a qualitative approach to gathering information that is both inductive and naturalistic.

Focus groups have been found useful prior to, during, and after programs, events, or experiences. They have been helpful in assessing needs, generating information for constructing questionnaires, developing plans, recruiting new clientele, finding out how customers make decisions to use or not use a product or service, testing new programs and ideas, improving existing programs, and evaluating outcomes.

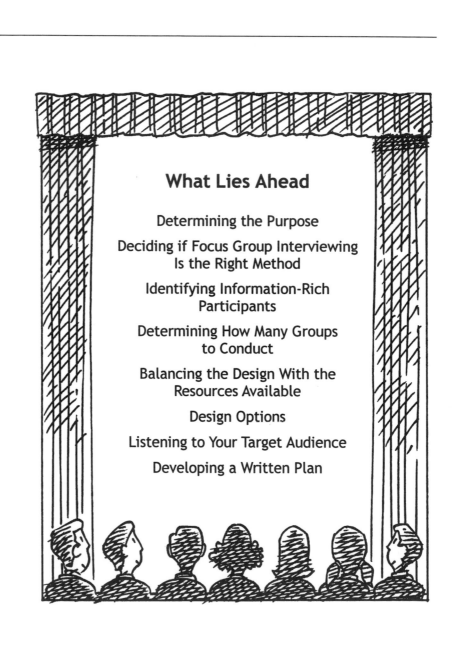

What Lies Ahead

Determining the Purpose

Deciding if Focus Group Interviewing
Is the Right Method

Identifying Information-Rich
Participants

Determining How Many Groups
to Conduct

Balancing the Design With the
Resources Available

Design Options

Listening to Your Target Audience

Developing a Written Plan

2

Planning the Focus Group Study

Planning is a task of making sure everyone on the team agrees about the purpose and expected outcomes of a study and then balancing what might be nice to do with what can be done with the resources available. We commit our thoughts to paper and invite others to provide feedback. It forces us to go beyond our own thinking and seek the insights of colleagues. Successful planning keeps promises reasonable, timelines efficient but doable, and budgets balanced. Think of the plan as an investment that prevents costly mistakes.

Determining the Purpose

Planning is crucial, but sometimes people quickly skip over it. In fact, people often begin focus group studies by drafting questions. It is better to back up, think about the purpose, and ask some fundamental questions.

At times, the request for the study originates from someone relatively unfamiliar with focus group interviews. For example, a director of an educational organization might want to find out how to reach new clientele, a curriculum coordinator might want to test out ideas for new programs, or a coordinator of county human services may want to get residents' perceptions of the organization. When the idea or request for a study is handed to a research unit, researchers often need more information on the nature of the problem, what information is being requested, and how the information will be used. Failure to clarify the problem can result in a study that misses the mark.

We begin planning by meeting with the person requesting the study, and we encourage this person to bring along several colleagues.

Typically it involves people who will be on the research team and people who will be responsible for doing something with the results. This meeting often includes two to seven people. We begin by having the people in the meeting discuss questions such as the following:

- What is the problem that the study is to address?
- What led up to the decision to do this study?
- What is the purpose of the study?
- What kinds of information do you want?
- What types of information are of particular importance?
- Who wants the information? (Or, to whom do you want to give the information?)
- How will you use the information? (Or, what do you want them to do with the information?)

The goal is for us to clearly understand what the client wants and to make sure the people requesting the study agree on the nature of the problem and the types of information needed to address the problem. Sometimes we will work on projects in which decision makers are extremely clear about what they want, why they want it, and what they intend to do with it. These meetings are straightforward. Other times, the meetings are messier, and it takes more effort to arrive at agreement on the purpose of the study. This happens when the people requesting the study have different visions of the purpose of the study, the kind of information they want, and what they intend to do with the information. This is particularly true when working on community issues. For example, after several fatal drinking and driving accidents, a group of community members came together to do something about "the problem." But people didn't agree on what the problem was. Was it drinking? Or was it drinking and driving? Some people thought the purpose of the study was to get information to help design programs to decrease teenage drinking and driving, but others felt the purpose should be to design programs to decrease teenage drinking. These different purposes would take the study in different directions. If the decision makers aren't in agreement about the purpose of the study, someone is going to be disappointed with the results.

It may be beneficial to ask why the information is needed in several different ways. For example, "Tell me about the background of the proposed study." "What prompted you to consider the study?" "Who is interested in the study results?" "What might those individuals do with the study results?" This pattern of questioning lets the researcher get a better picture of the information needs of intended users and thereby keep the study on target. It can also help highlight differences and similarities in people's thinking about the study. Sometimes the researcher's role is to help people see differences in their thinking about the project and come to agreement. Hidden agendas, organizational politics, and fuzzy thinking are obstacles to achieving agreement.

Two dangers regularly occur in the public and nonprofit environments. Be watchful of them. First, don't be surprised if the sponsors are unclear or fuzzy about what they want, especially in exploratory studies. It sometimes takes time and several meetings to clarify the purpose. Second, the sponsor may have exaggerated expectations of what can reasonably be delivered.

Deciding If Focus Group Interviewing Is the Right Method

Once you determine the purpose, you can begin thinking about what methods to use. People come to us and say they want to do focus groups. After talking with them about the purpose of their study and the resources they have, we sometimes recommend that they use another method of data collection that is better suited for their situation. Just because someone wants to do focus groups doesn't mean it's a good idea.

Before launching a focus group study, it may be helpful to think about when focus groups work well and when they don't.

When to Use Focus Group Interviews

Focus group interviews should be considered when:

- You are looking for the range of ideas or feelings that people have about something.

- You are trying to understand differences in perspectives between groups or categories of people. Often, people in power see a situation or issue differently from those who are not. Professional people (medical, educational, scientific, technical, business, legal) often lose touch with the very people they are trying to serve. And top management often sees issues differently than frontline providers do. These differences can cause major problems, particularly when they aren't recognized and understood.

- The purpose is to uncover factors that influence opinions, behavior, or motivation. Focus groups can provide insight into complicated topics when opinions are conditional or when the area of concern relates to multifaceted behavior or motivation. Under what conditions would a health care provider admit a mistake? What factors influence a new mom's willingness to have a home visit from a public health nurse?

- You want ideas to emerge from the group. A group possesses the capacity to become more than the sum of its parts, to exhibit a synergy that individuals alone don't possess.

- You want to pilot test ideas, materials, plans, or policies.

- The researcher needs information to design a large-scale quantitative study. Focus groups have provided researchers with valuable insights into conducting complicated quantitative investigations. What words do people use to talk about this issue? What do they see as the range of options for answering a question?

- The researcher needs information to help shed light on quantitative data already collected.

- The clients or intended audience places high value on capturing the comments or language used by the target audience.

When Not to Use Focus Group Interviews

Focus group interviews should *not* be considered when:

- You want people to come to consensus.
- You want to educate people.
- You don't intend to use the results but instead want to give the appearance of listening.
- You are asking for sensitive information that should not be shared in a group or could be harmful to someone if it is shared in a group.
- You need statistical projections. Findings from a focus group study can't be used to make statistical projections. There aren't enough participants involved, and sampling isn't done in a way to support projections.
- The environment is emotionally charged, and a group discussion is likely to intensify the conflict. This is likely to occur in situations where the people are polarized on an issue, trust has deteriorated, and the participants are confrontational.
- The researcher has lost control over critical aspects of the study. When control is relinquished to other individuals or groups, the study may be prone to manipulation and bias or just poor practice. The researcher should maintain control over critical aspects such as participant selection, question development, and analysis protocol. This will be a constant challenge when conducting focus groups in a participatory mode within communities. For more discussion on this, see *Involving Community Members in Focus Groups* (Krueger & King, 1998).
- Other methodologies can produce better quality information.
- Other methodologies can produce the same quality information more economically.
- You can't ensure the confidentiality of sensitive information.

Identifying Information-Rich Participants

Another part of planning is figuring out what types of people could give you the information you want. Who are the target audiences? At this point, we aren't thinking of names of individuals; we are thinking of what characteristics the people should have. For example, suppose an educational institution is interested in how customers perceive current programs. On the surface, this appears straightforward; just talk to students. But it may be more complex. Are decision makers interested in current students, students who have tried the programs and left, potential students, or businesses that hire their students? Are the perceptions of students with certain demographic characteristics more critical than others for this study? A precise definition of the customers is essential to get the needed information.

It sometimes helps to think of this as identifying the "information-rich" cases. Patton (1990) describes these information-rich cases as "those from which one can learn a great deal about the issues of central importance to the purpose of the research" (p. 169). The question the researcher asks is, "Who has the greatest amount of insight on this topic?" In the example above, potential customers—perhaps people who requested information but never actually participated in the program—may not know many specifics about the program. However, they would be rich with information about their perceptions of the program, what keeps them from participating, or what might get them to participate.

In some studies, several different types of people can give you information from different perspectives. For example, a public health agency and a school were working together to figure out what it would take to get elementary schoolchildren to eat more fruits and vegetables while at school. They conducted focus groups with parents, teachers, food service workers, and second- and fourth-grade students. Each type of participant was able to give a different view of the problem and potential solutions.

Determining How Many Groups to Conduct

The rule of thumb is, plan three or four focus groups with any one type of participant. Once you have conducted these, determine if you have reached saturation. *Saturation* is a term used to describe the point when you have heard the range of ideas and aren't getting new information. If you were still getting new information after three or four groups, you would conduct more groups. The reason you plan three to four groups is because focus groups are analyzed across groups. The analyst looks for patterns and themes across groups.

TIP

Think About the Final Report: What Type of People Do You Want to Be Able to Say Something About?

When trying to figure out how to configure focus groups, think about what type of people you want to be able to say something about in your final report. Do you want to be able to say something about how new moms feel about a program, or is it important to be able to say how new moms who are teenagers feel versus new moms who are older than thirty? If you just want to say something about how new moms feel, you could do three to four groups with various kinds of new moms. But if it is important to be able to compare and contrast perceptions of new moms based on age, you would complete at least three groups with each age category you select. It would get even more complicated if it were also important to know how moms of different races or ethnicities feel about the program. Or do you want to be able to talk about how dads feel about the program? Thinking about the final report may seem premature at this stage, but it really helps clarify the type of information needed from different types of people.

If you want to be able to compare and contrast how certain types of people talk about an issue, you must separate these people into different groups. For example, if we wanted to know how men's and women's opinions were similar or different on a certain issue, we would conduct three groups with men and three groups with women. That way, we can analyze across the men's groups, analyze across the women's groups, and then compare and contrast the findings. If we mixed men and women in the same groups, it would be much more difficult to analyze based on gender.

Also, when planning groups, we avoid mixing people who may feel they have different levels of expertise or power related to the issue. We want to create an environment where all participants feel comfortable saying what they think or feel. If there is a power differential, some participants may be reluctant to talk. When structuring groups, we probably wouldn't include supervisors and their employees in the same group. We probably wouldn't include teachers and students or teachers and parents in the same groups. We probably wouldn't mix seventh-grade boys with eleventh-grade boys. We are saying probably because our experience tells us that in most cases, it isn't a good idea, but we wouldn't say that we would never do these things. Again, the study and situation would dictate what we would do.

You can see that the number of groups could grow rapidly. Recently, a state agency was interested in finding out how people with diabetes from different communities of color felt about their diabetes, how they coped with the disease, and what they thought their health care providers could do to help them stay healthy. The agency conducted sixteen groups—four focus groups with each of the following types of people: African Americans, American Indians, Hispanics, and Southeast Asians. This decision came after considerable discussion about the pros and cons of additional subdivisions, such as urban versus rural, or for separating participants by country of origin, by language or dialect, by fluency in English, and so on. Each decision influenced resources needed, the timeline required, and the skills needed by the research team.

Also, consider the more traditional ways of dividing people into categories. Factors such as geographic location, age, gender, income, participation characteristics, family size, and employment status can be helpful ways to identify who should participate in focus groups. The decision of whom to involve must be related to the purpose of the study.

Nonprofit and service organizations typically have three categories of people who are of special importance to listen to—advisory groups, employees, and clients. Each of these can be subdivided into categories. These organizations often conduct focus groups with clients to find out how to design new programs or services but forget to ask frontline employees for their input about what it will take to make the program or service work.

Balancing the Design With the Resources Available

We talk about what is doable with the time and resources available for the study. Often, planning is a balancing act between what would be nice to do and what is doable with the resources at hand. Resources include the time available for the project, the financial resources available, and the talent and creativity of people on the study team. If resources are limited, fewer groups can be conducted. Usually, we are working with not-for-profit groups in which financial resources are limited. In contrast, just because resources are plentiful doesn't mean one should conduct more groups. We have heard of organizations that have conducted sixty, seventy, or eighty focus groups on one topic using the same questions. In our opinion, that's a waste of time and money.

Seldom do we conduct more than thirty groups on a topic, even for national studies.

Think about what is an appropriate amount of resources to spend on a project. Try to fit the resources to the decision to be made. One can usually conduct fewer groups when there is little risk to making the decision (i.e., the decision is easily reversible, people won't be seriously affected by the change, it doesn't involve big expenditures). If the decision involves a great deal of risk, one would increase the number of focus groups and consider enhancing the study with quantitative data.

Often, we decide how many groups can be conducted with the resources available and then decide how we should configure the groups. If we have the resources to conduct ten groups, how many different types of participants (or target audiences) should we listen to? How many groups should we conduct with each type of participant? What configuration will give us the most useful information?

Here is an example. In the study designed to find out how to get kids to eat more fruits and vegetables while at school, there were enough resources to conduct twelve groups at the pilot elementary school. The planners decided it was most important to listen to the kids because they had the most information about what it would take to get them to eat more fruits and vegetables. They decided to conduct three groups with second graders and three groups with fourth graders. They also knew that input from food service workers was crucial to making changes. There was only a handful of food service workers in the school, so they could all participate in one group. The planners

also wanted to hear from teachers and parents. They decided to conduct two groups with teachers and three groups with parents.

Expect to struggle with the design a bit. It takes time to figure out how to configure the groups.

Design Options

Single-Category Design

The traditional design for a focus group study is to conduct focus groups until you have reached the point of theoretical saturation—the point when you are not gaining new insights. The number of groups needed to reach saturation can vary, but usually the researcher will initially plan for three or four focus groups with a target audience and then decide if adequate saturation has been reached or if additional groups should be conducted.

Although theoretical saturation is a great concept and useful in academic work, as a consultant you won't land many contracts if you say you plan to conduct groups until you reach theoretical saturation.

EXAMPLE

Example of Single-Category Design

Let's say you wanted to use focus groups to evaluate a leadership development program for youth. You decide the information-rich people are youth who have completed the program in the past two years. You don't want to compare or contrast based on any other features. So you use a single-category design. You conduct three or four groups with your target audience and determine if saturation is achieved. If saturation is achieved, then the study is completed and reports are prepared. However, if new information is being obtained after the third or fourth group, the researcher will need to decide if additional groups should be held or if the report should indicate that saturation was not achieved. Perhaps it is enough to know that people hold widely different views on the topic.

	Number of Groups (O = 1 group)			
Audience (youth who completed the program in the past 2 years) Saturation?	O	O	O	O

Figure 2.1.   Single-Category Design

Clients want to know how many groups are needed, how long the study will take, and how much it will cost. Few clients will give you a blank check to conduct as many groups as needed until saturation is achieved. Therefore, we typically plan at least three or four groups for the most important groups we want to listen to.

Multiple-Category Design

A variation of the traditional design is to conduct groups with several audiences, either sequentially or simultaneously. This design allows the researcher to make comparisons in two ways—from one group to another within a category (youth) and from one category to another category (e.g., comparing what youth said to what parents said).

EXAMPLE

Example of a Multiple-Category Design

Let's continue the above example but make it more complex. Let's say it is important to hear the reactions of youth who have completed the program, as well as parents of youth who have completed the program, mentors involved in the program, and staff members. It is important to be able to compare and contrast the reactions of these different groups. Let's suppose that you have enough resources to conduct only ten groups.

You believe feedback from youth and parents will be most useful for your study, so you place more emphasis on getting information from them. You conduct four groups with youth because their feedback is most important. But you divide the youth groups by age, knowing that younger youth are often intimidated by older youth or simply defer to them. You conduct three groups with parents. It is important but not critical to get feedback from both mentors and staff. You decide to conduct two groups with mentors. There are so few staff members that you are able to get their input in one focus group.

	Number of Groups (O = 1 group)		
Audience 1 (youth, ages 14-15)	O	O	
(youth, ages 16-18)	O	O	
Audience 2 (parents)	O	O	O
Audience 3 (mentors)	O	O	
Audience 4 (staff)	O		

Figure 2.2.   Multiple-Category Design

Double-Layer Design

Another version of the traditional design involves multiple layers, which might involve geographic areas as the first layer and different audiences as the second layer. In this design, the researchers can make comparisons between any of the layers in the design.

EXAMPLE

Example of a Double-Layer Design

Suppose that a nationwide health service wants to do a study to better understand what patients suffering from severe depression consider to be good health care. The results of the study are to be used, along with numerous other sources of data, to develop clinical guidelines for care of patients who suffer from depression. The study team decides it is most important to talk with patients who are being treated for depression but are not currently hospitalized. They also want to listen to family members who are close to these patients. This might include spouses, parents, or adult children of patients. The health service has four geographic regions, and studies traditionally have included all four regions. One facility is selected to participate in each region.

Layer 1	Layer 2	Number of Groups (O = 1 group)		
East				
	Audience 1 (patients)	O	O	O
	Audience 2 (family members)	O		
West				
	Audience 1 (patients)	O	O	O
	Audience 2 (family members)	O		
South				
	Audience 1 (patients)	O	O	O
	Audience 2 (family members)	O		
North				
	Audience 1 (patients)	O	O	O
	Audience 2 (family members)	O		

Figure 2.3. Double-Layer Design

Broad-Involvement Design

Occasionally there are studies with widespread public interest. In these studies, some people may be concerned if they are left out of the study. A potential sampling strategy is to identify a primary audience who is considered to be your greatest information-rich source. We'll call this source your "target audience," whereas other sources represent

EXAMPLE

Example of a Broad-Involvement Design

Let's say a state department of education is proposing policy changes in special education. They want to know what kind of implications the proposed changes may have for what takes place in the classroom. The proposed changes directly affect special education teachers; therefore, the study team believes special education teachers are the people who can best provide the needed information—how the changes will affect the classroom. Yet, the team knows that other people can also provide feedback: regular education teachers, parents, students, advocates, and school administrators. In some studies, particularly in the public sector, there are groups that feel they must be listened to before decisions are made or policy is established. These groups may feel that the study would be incomplete unless their views are heard and recorded. The study

team may agree that listening to these groups would enhance findings, but they have limited time and resources. In these situations, the strategy begins with your primary audience (special education teachers), and the team listens broadly to establish a clear baseline. Perhaps the study team conducts one group with special education teachers in each of seven education districts in the state. Then one or two focus groups are conducted with each of the additional audiences (regular education teachers, parents, students, advocates, and administrators). Results of these groups are compared back to the baseline established by special education teachers. Occasionally, unique and crucial information may emerge from the focus groups with these secondary audiences. Then additional focus groups can be conducted with that audience.

	Number of Groups (O = I group)						
Audience I (special education teachers)	O	O	O	O	O	O	O
Audience 2 (regular education teachers)	O	O					
Audience 3 (parents)	O						
Audience 4 (students)	O						
Audience 5 (advocates)	O						
Audience 6 (administrators)	O						

Figure 2.4. Broad-Involvement Design

secondary but important perspectives. For example, in a program to prevent teen violence, researchers decided that their target audience was male teenagers, ages thirteen to seventeen, living in high-crime neighborhoods. Other audiences (police, teachers, parents) may have had valuable perspectives on violence prevention, but resources prevented an in-depth study of all audience categories. However, if the study listened only to the target audience, other audiences may not have cooperated in developing solution strategies. In some environments, there is the attitude that if my "group" isn't involved, then we're not considered important when it comes time to work toward a solution. Or, "I can't believe it because you never listened to people like me!" In this design, you are concerned not only about what is good research but also about what it will take to get people to buy into your project and support your efforts. You start by making sure you have good research, then you add groups to make sure the study is practical in a political sense.

The design strategy consists of first anchoring the study with the groups of the target audience. In fact, this audience is often purposefully oversampled and exceeds the point of saturation. This is often done to include geographic representation (e.g., a state agency wants one group done in each of its seven regions). After the patterns are detected within the target audience, later analysis compares each additional audience type back to the target audience. If a particular audience provides key information that is not included in the analysis of the target audience, then the researcher might add a second or third group to that particular secondary audience to determine if that pattern appears again in similar groups.

Listening to Your Target Audience

Once you have a plan in mind, seek out and visit with several people who have the characteristics of your target audience. For example, if you're going to listen to special education teachers, find some special education teachers and get their advice on your plan. (It would be even better to have a special education teacher or two on your research team. But if that isn't possible, make sure to do this step.) Perhaps share a meal with them and ask their advice on how to undertake the study. Describe the study and ask questions such as the following:

..., so, what would it take to get you to come to these discussions?

- How can we get the names of people like this?
- How do we find people like this?
- How are people in this general category alike or different? If we want to invite people who feel the same way, what advice do you have?
- What would it take to get people to come to a discussion like this?
- Who should invite people to participate?
- When would it be easiest for these people to come? (Time of day, day of week, etc.)
- Where would be the best place to hold the discussion?
- What would be some good questions to ask?
- What do you think of these questions? (Try out a few questions.)
- What kind of person should ask the questions (moderate)?

Listen. You're trying to find out what it will take to make this study work. You are looking for pitfalls or roadblocks. This is really important if you are working with an audience with which you are unfamiliar. Perhaps you want to conduct focus groups with migrant workers or teenagers who smoke or men with prostate problems. The sponsoring agency should have connections with individuals in the target audience. Have them introduce you. Ask the types of questions listed above. It is amazing what you can learn.

Developing a Written Plan

After we have discussed the purpose, talked about who to listen to, and gotten advice from people like the audiences we want to listen to, we develop a written plan. The value of the written plan is threefold. First, it forces the researcher to think through the study in a logical manner and clarify ideas. Ideas that make sense in our discussions sometimes have glaring shortcomings when placed on paper. Second, the written plan allows decision makers to provide feedback. Written plans can be circulated and discussed more readily than our thoughts. Plans can also highlight differences in understanding—such as different views of the purpose of a project—before the project goes too far. The plan helps

TIP

Ask for Help

Early in the planning process, you will need ideas. Invite a small group of researchers or clients to discuss options and choices about the study. This discussion could involve more than one meeting and, at times, will become a brainstorming session. Avoid locking in on specifics too early. Talk about the purpose of the study, whether focus groups are appropriate, the types of people who can give you the information you need (target audiences), how many focus groups to conduct, and the resources available.

us make sure everyone is in agreement and that we understand the client's needs. Third, plans ensure that adequate resources and time are available to obtain needed information.

We include the purpose, background information, types of information needed, target audiences, plan of action, products or deliverables, timeline, and budget. A timeline should contain the following elements: dates, steps, people responsible, people assisting, and comments. The timeline presents the sequence of steps and identifies which tasks are to be completed by which team members. Administrators have regularly criticized evaluators and researchers for not respecting the time requirements of decision making. At some point a decision will be made, regardless of whether the results are available. The timeline provides decision makers with a timetable for information—a timetable that must be prepared in advance and then respected by both the researcher and the decision maker.

The plan should be shared with colleagues, particularly those who are familiar with the issue or program being studied. It is also helpful to share it with colleagues or professionals familiar with focus group interviewing procedures. When we ask others to review the plan, we ask them to point out areas where things could go wrong—aspects that are illogical, impractical, or unclear.

SUMMARY

Don't overlook the critical importance of planning. The planning process begins by identifying the purpose of the study. Then we decide if focus group interviewing is the right method for the study. If it is, we identify information-rich target audiences and decide on the number of focus groups to be conducted. Idealistic designs are easy. Far more difficult is the challenge of developing an effective design using scarce resources. Feedback from colleagues, researchers, clients, and your target audience helps you identify problems before they occur.

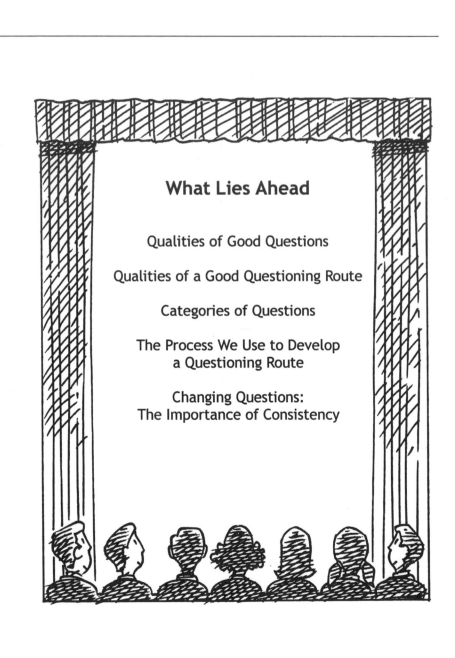

What Lies Ahead

Qualities of Good Questions

Qualities of a Good Questioning Route

Categories of Questions

The Process We Use to Develop
a Questioning Route

Changing Questions:
The Importance of Consistency

3

Developing a Questioning Route

The mother thought her daughter should have a comprehensive checkup before starting kindergarten. She made an appointment with an eminent psychologist to examine the youngster for any possible abnormal tendencies. Among the questions, the man of science asked, "Are you a boy or a girl?" "A boy," the little girl answered. Somewhat startled, the psychologist tried again. "When you grow up, are you going to be a woman or a man?" "A man," the little girl answered. On the way home, the mother asked, "Why did you make such strange replies to what the psychologist asked?" In a serious tone, the little girl replied, "He asked such silly questions, I thought he wanted silly answers!"

Developing good questions seems like it should be easy. But this is one of the areas where budding (and experienced) focus group researchers run into problems. Often beginners generate interesting questions, but it isn't clear how answers to those questions will help achieve the purpose of the study. Or they phrase the questions in ways that don't beg for discussion. A simple yes or no will do. Or they generate a list of thirty questions to be answered in a two-hour group. Developing good focus group questions requires time, help from buddies, and attention to a few guidelines.

The series of questions used in a focused interview—the questioning route—looks deceptively simple. Typically, a focused interview will include about a dozen questions for a two-hour group. If you asked these questions in an individual interview, the respondent could probably tell you everything he or she could think of related to the questions in just a few minutes. But when these questions are asked in a group environment, the discussion can last for several hours. Part of the reason is in the nature of the questions and the cognitive processes of humans. As participants answer questions, their responses spark ideas from other participants. Comments provide mental cues that trigger memories or thoughts of other participants—cues that help explore the range of perceptions.

Qualities of Good Questions

Good focus group questions have the following qualities.

Sound Conversational

The focus group is a social experience, and conversational questions help create and maintain an informal environment.

Use Words the Participants Would Use When Talking About the Issue

Don't use acronyms, jargon, and technical lingo unless you are talking to a group of experts. Professionals are sometimes held captive by their

language and inadvertently use technical terms or jargon that sound highfalutin and confuse and put off lay audiences. To avoid this, have the questions reviewed by people similar to your target audience to make sure the language is clear and unpretentious.

Are Easy to Say

Good questions are written so the moderator won't stumble over words or phrases. Some questions are great in written form but are awkward or stilted when asked orally.

Are Clear

When the question is asked, participants should understand what you're asking. This sounds pretty basic, but it is surprising how confusing some questions are. Sometimes moderators give long pre-ambles to questions, offer lengthy background, or use a long segue from one topic to another. Instead of clarifying the question, this can actually be confusing. Listeners may key on trivial phrases or words intended to build the case for the question, but these same phrases and words can confuse the focus group participant or take the discussion off on a tangent. Again, the question might be clear when one is reading it off the page but confusing when one hears it. When questions are unclear, either they don't make sense to the participant or they can be interpreted in different ways.

Are Usually Short

Lengthy questions can be confusing to respondents. Participants have a hard time distinguishing the core intent of the question. In general, you reduce clarity as the length of the question increases.

Are Usually Open-Ended

Open-ended questions are a hallmark of focus group interviewing. These questions imply that a few words or a phrase are insufficient as an answer. They beg for explanations, descriptions, or illustrations.

Are Usually One-Dimensional

Inadvertently, moderators might include words that they think are synonyms, but they're seen as entirely different concepts by participants. Although the moderator means well, the participants get confused. For example, "How was the program useful and practical to you?" For some, "useful" and "practical" may be very different concepts. Other times, moderators might add a second sentence or phrase that supposedly amplifies the question but confuses the respondents because it introduces another dimension. For example, "Which of these is most important to you? Or which should be acted on first?" Again, the moderator assumed that what was important should be acted on first, but this may not be the view of participants.

Include Clear, Well-Thought-Out Directions

When asking participants to do something, be sure to provide clear instructions. For example, if you are asking participants to list something, do you want them to write it down on paper before they discuss? How much time should they take? Practice the instructions whenever the tasks are complicated, such as when using small breakout groups or activities that have multiple steps.

Qualities of a Good Questioning Route

A questioning route is a list of sequenced questions in complete, conversational sentences. A good questioning route:

Has an Easy Beginning

Good focus groups get off to a fast, conversational start. Tough questions at the very beginning take too much time and may be modified by later comments in the group. Use questions that are easy for everyone in the group to answer.

Is Sequenced

It is called a focus group because it has a focus. One part of the focus is the question sequence. The questions naturally flow from one question to another. By contrast, it is not a bunch of questions just thrown together. There is thought given to the sequence.

BACKGROUND

Questioning Route versus Topic Guide

There are two different questioning strategies used by focus group moderators: topic guide and questioning route. The topic guide is like an outline with a list of topics or issues to be pursued in the focus group. This list consists of words or phrases that remind the moderator of the topic. By contrast, the questioning route is a sequence of questions in complete sentences. The topic guide tends to be used by professional moderators in marketing research studies, whereas the questioning route is often preferred in the public/nonprofit and aca-demic environments. The advantages and dis-advantages of each approach are described in Chapter 2 of *Developing Questions for Focus Groups*. We prefer the questioning route be-cause it fosters consistency in questioning and, as a result, improves analysis. It forces the moderator or research team to think about the words and phrases to be used ahead of time, and it helps the sponsor more clearly understand what will occur in the focus group. In addition, it increases consistency in the way questions are asked across groups.

Moves From General to Specific

Another reason that this process is called a focus group is that the questions move from broad and general questions (often of lesser importance) to more specific questions of greater importance to the study.

Uses the Time Available Wisely

It is always a challenge to anticipate how much time is needed to answer the questions. The moderator must allow sufficient time for the important questions that are being asked during the latter part of the focus group. The question route provides the roadmap with "mile markers." This is discussed later in the section on estimating time for questions.

Categories of Questions

Not all questions are equal. Different types of questions are used during the focus group. Each type of question has a distinct purpose.

Some questions exist only to help people get prepared to answer a more important question. The moderator may move through some questions rapidly but spend significant time on others. The level of importance influences the amount of time spent on the question as well as the intensity of the analysis. Not all questions are analyzed in the same way. Some questions, such as the opening question, may not be analyzed at all.

Essentially there are five categories of questions, each with a distinctive function in the flow of a focus group interview. We call these question categories opening, introductory, transition, key, and ending.

Opening Questions

The intent of the opening question is not to get profound information but rather to get people talking and to help people feel comfortable. All participants are asked to answer this question, going one by one around the table. We want everyone to talk early in the discussion because the longer it is before a person says something in a group, the less likely he or she is to say something.

The opening question is designed to be easy to answer. And it should be easy to answer quickly (usually within thirty seconds). Usually, it is best to ask for facts as opposed to attitudes or opinions of participants at this point. Questions of attitude or opinion take time to answer, require examples or stories, and beg for discussion. The opening question is not a discussion question but strictly a process of getting everyone to talk early in the group. Opening questions typically aren't analyzed.

It is important that the question not highlight power or status differences among participants. We don't ask teenagers how old they are or what grade they are in because young people are very sensitive to age differences. We don't ask occupation or level of education. We don't ask farmers the size of their farming operation. We don't want to emphasize differences because some people may simply defer to others in the group who they feel are older, wiser, more experienced, or whatever.

Introductory Questions

Introductory questions introduce the topic of discussion and get people to start thinking about their connection with the topic. These questions encourage conversation among participants. Typically, these are open-ended questions that allow participants to tell about how they see or

EXAMPLE

Opening Question

One of the best opening questions that we've seen was used with dentists. It was: "Tell us who you are, where you practice dentistry, and what you most enjoy doing when you're not practicing dentistry." The question was easy to answer and established that all participants had dentistry in common, that they were practitioners, and that they were human beings with interests, hobbies, and families.

understand the issue, service, or product under investigation. Sometimes the introductory question asks participants to remember when they first experienced or encountered the organization or topic under investigation and to describe the experience. Or a question could ask people to describe how they use a product or service. Or, "What is the first thing that comes to mind when you hear the phrase . . . ?" Introductory questions begin to give the moderator clues about participants' views.

Transition Questions

Transition questions move the conversation into the key questions that drive the study. They serve as the logical link between the introductory questions and the key questions. During these questions, the participants are becoming aware of how others view the topic. These questions set the stage for productive key questions. Often transition questions ask participants to go into more depth than introductory questions about their experiences and use of a product. Although the introductory question surfaces the topic, the transition questions make the connection between the participant and the topic of investigation.

Key Questions

Key questions drive the study. Typically, there are two to five questions in this category. These are usually the first questions to be developed by the research team and the ones that require the greatest attention in the analysis. It's important for the moderator to know which questions are key questions. The moderator needs to allow sufficient time for a full discussion of these questions. Although only a few minutes might be allocated for each of the earlier questions, the key questions may need as much as ten or twenty minutes each. Furthermore, the moderator will likely need to use pauses and probes more frequently with key questions. Key questions usually begin about one third to one half of the way into the focus group.

Ending Questions

These questions bring closure to the discussion, enable participants to reflect on previous comments, and are critical to analysis. Three types of ending questions are valuable: the all-things-considered question, the summary question, and the final question.

The all-things-considered question is used to determine the final position of participants on critical areas of concern. This question allows each participant to reflect on all comments shared in the discussion and then identify which aspects are most important, most in need of action, and so on. Also, an individual may have shared inconsistent points of view, and this question allows him or her to clarify a position at the conclusion of the discussion. Often we ask each person in the group to answer this question. Examples include the following: "Suppose you had one minute to talk to the governor on the topic of merit pay. What would you say?" or "Of all the needs we discussed, which one is most important to you?"

This all-things-considered question is helpful in analysis because it is used to interpret conflicting comments and assign weight to what was said. Sometimes trivial concerns are talked about frequently during the focus group, but it's a serious mistake when the analyst assumes that frequency reflects importance. If the analyst wants to know what participants consider important, then the moderator must ask that question, and it is ideal to use it as an ending question.

The summary question is asked after the moderator or assistant moderator has given a short oral summary (two or three minutes) of the discussion evoked by the key questions. After the summary, the participants are asked about the adequacy of the summary. This question also plays a critical role in analysis. The question can be asked in several ways, such as, "Is this an adequate summary?" or "Did I correctly describe what was said?" or "How well does that capture what was said here?"

The final question in a focus group is an insurance question. Its unique purpose is to ensure that critical aspects have not been overlooked. The question begins with a short overview of the purpose of the study. This overview may be slightly longer and more descriptive than what was said in the advance letter or oral introduction to the focus group. Following this overview, the moderator asks the final question: "Have we missed anything?" or "Is there anything that we should have talked about but didn't?"

Save time for this question or it won't work. It is best to have about ten minutes remaining before the promised adjournment time. This question is particularly important at the beginning of a series of focus groups to ensure that the questioning route is logical and complete. This final question also can be used to get feedback on your moderating skills. If something isn't working, the participants are often willing to tell you if you ask with a smile and explain that you want to improve. We sometimes explain, "This is the first in a series of groups like this that we are doing. Do you have any advice for how we can improve?"

EXAMPLE

A Questioning Route

Here is the questioning route used in focus groups with parents. These parents had recently been involved with an intensive family therapy program.

Opening:	1. Tell us your name and tell us how long you have been working with (name of program).
Introductory:	2. How did you learn about the service?
Transition:	3. Think back to when you first became involved with these services. What were your first impressions?
	4. What was the startup process like for you?
Key Questions:	5. What was particularly helpful about the services you received?
	6. What was particularly frustrating about the services?
	7. Is your child any different because he or she received these services? If so, how?
	8. Is your family life any different because you received these services? If so, how?
Ending Questions:	9. If you had a chance to give advice to the director of this program, what advice would you give?
	10. We wanted you to help us evaluate these services. We want to know how to improve the service and what difference the service makes to kids and families. Is there anything that we missed? Is there anything that you came wanting to say that you didn't get a chance to say?

Questions That Engage Participants

Up to now, we've shown you examples of questions that only required people to talk. We also ask people to do things—list, draw, review, cut and paste, debate. There are several benefits to creating activities and experiences that get people to do something other than talk. These questions often tap into a different part of the brain or heart. With some, you get away from linear or rational answers. Some provide wonderful images and symbolism. Also, participants often have fun with these.

Listing Things

Perhaps the easiest way to engage people in a different way is to ask them to make a list. This is often done with a flip chart or chalkboard so participants can remember what has already been said. There are several ways that the list can be prepared. One way is to have participants verbally offer ideas as the moderator or assistant moderator records these on the flip chart. Another way is to give participants several minutes to record their individual lists on paper provided to them and then tabulate results. The lists could be read aloud by the participants, read by the moderator, or sorted and read by the assistant moderator. This listing process helps identify duplicate items. The listing process also affords the participants a few moments to reflect before they offer an answer. Consider these examples: "Think back to when you had awful service. What makes customer service terrible? Write your answers on a piece of paper. In a moment we'll share these with each other." Or, "On the paper in front of you, jot down three characteristics of successful youth workers."

The list can be used simply to identify the range of responses. Or, the list can be used to move to a higher level. After the group has generated a list in response to "What makes customer service terrible?" the moderator can refer to the list and ask each person, "Which item do you consider to be the most important on the list?" or "If you had to pick one thing from this list that is most important to you, what would it be?" Then the moderator could focus the following discussion on the items that the participants chose as most important.

CAUTION

Flip Charts Can Slow the Conversation

We use flip charts sparingly in focus groups because it can stifle conversation. People can talk much faster than a recorder can write. Often participants will stop talking so the recorder can list an idea. Also, people tend to offer phrases that are easy to list, rather than offering long examples, which are usually much more useful during analysis. The moderator must continually encourage people to give examples or explain or share more as he or she captures information on the chart. Also, listing items on the flip chart tends to put the emphasis back on the moderator. Participants serially talk to the moderator rather than responding to each other. It becomes the moderator's conversation, rather than the group's conversation. Therefore, we usually don't use a flip chart to record items on more than two questions in a group.

Rating Items

Rating scales can help identify which items should be discussed in more detail. Usually the researchers develop the criteria and the rating scale. The rating exercise should be simple, and participants should be able to complete it within a few minutes. Consequently, there is a limit to the number of items that can be rated.

EXAMPLE

Examples of Response Categories

When using a rating exercise in a focus group select scales that are common. For example:

very satisfied	*excellent*	*strongly agree*
satisfied	*good*	*agree*
dissatisfied	*fair*	*neutral*
very dissatisfied	*poor*	*disagree*
		strongy disagree

At times there is value in asking participants to help develop the items to be rated. In these situations, keep the response scale constant, but have participants identify the items to be rated. The researcher can then compare ratings of items and array these from high to low.

Suppose we are interested in how customers rate a local restaurant. We could use an instrument previously developed by the restaurant, and if we did so, we could compare results to earlier findings. But the predetermined criteria might miss some critical elements of customer concern. Most often these rating forms ask about quality of food, quantity of food, speed of service, friendliness of service, and so on. Suppose, however, that areas of greater concern to customers are parking lot congestion, food prices, presence or absence of smoking areas, or noisiness. We suggest that you weigh the pros and cons of having criteria determined by the researcher versus criteria developed by participants. An advantage of using criteria developed by each person is that you get closer to their reality. The disadvantage is that these are sometimes difficult to analyze across groups because each group might be rating a different set of items.

Here is an example used with students in a high school: "We'd like you to develop a report card for your school. You're familiar with grades, A, B, C, D, and F, that you get for school subjects like English, history, and algebra. We want you to make a report card for your school, but you get to pick the subjects or the areas and you get to give the grades. Pick subjects or things that are important to you. It could be something about people, the building, activities, or anything connected with the school. Pick subjects and give each subject a grade from A to F. So, each of you take one of these cards and make a report card for this school." Once the students were done, they shared their lists and grades, which were recorded on a flip chart. Then students were asked to pick out and discuss things that were rising to the top—getting A's. Then they were asked to pick those things that were failing. Students were then asked how the things that were failing could be improved.

When participants have completed the exercise, the ratings should then be discussed. If you aren't going to discuss the results, then do the rating before or after the focus group, and don't waste time having them complete it while the group is meeting. The follow-up discussion usually begins by asking each participant to share his or her ratings (or the results could be passed in and announced or tabulated without individual identification). Sometimes we use a flip chart to list results, and after participants have seen results from others, they may wish to amplify or even modify their response. Much of the value of the rating scale is in the follow-up discussion. "Are any categories missing?" "What do you feel most passionate about?" "What might be done to improve these items?"

Choosing Among Alternatives— Pilot Testing Ideas

This is a great use for focus groups. Participants are offered several choices, usually at least three but no more than five. The participants are then asked to look over the alternatives, talk about the advantages and disadvantages of each, discuss what they like and don't like, and select the one that they like the best. In addition to making the selection and announcing the choice, the participants also offer a reason for why they decided the way they did. This strategy is often used in selecting from among visual displays, advertising layouts, promotional or educational materials, logos, or even program options. We've used this strategy to evaluate different delivery options for higher education in a community, to review proposed social service programs, and to get feedback on different formats for educational materials. In some situations, the participants were given short descriptions to read. In others, participants watched short videos or reviewed materials or mockups. Participants discussed the options, asked questions, and then selected the one they preferred.

Picture Sort

The picture sort begins with a stack of pictures, typically from magazines. It might be a stack of pictures of women, men, or teens. The pictures depict different types of people doing a variety of things. The moderator asks the participants to sort through the pictures and pick out those that match certain characteristics. For example, "Look through these pictures and pick out the people who would participate in community education." "Here are some pictures of women. Sort the pictures into two categories. One category is women you think would breast-feed their child, and the second category is women who you think would bottle-feed their child." After the sorting exercise, the moderator asks participants to talk about what it was about the pictures that caused them to put them in certain categories. The images help us understand an issue in a different way from words.

Drawing a Picture

Each focus group participant is given a blank piece of paper and a pencil, markers, or crayons. He or she is then asked to draw a picture that might offer some insights on behavior or attitudes. Use stick figures for those anxious about the difficulty of drawing people. A variation is to hand out a "roughed-out" sketch and ask participants to add words or narrative to the pictures.

After each participant has drawn a picture, he or she is asked to hold it up for others to see and then describe it. When the group is finished sharing, the moderator might ask the group what they saw in the different approaches. What was similar? What was different?

EXAMPLE

Picture Drawing Questions

Here are examples of questions used to determine (1) the environment of an urban youth center, (2) new moms' images of an ideal home visit from a public health nurse, and (3) employee morale.

Example 1

We want you to draw someone who uses the youth center. Draw a picture of this person standing at the door of the youth center after having spent the evening there. Draw the person. (Give them some time.) This person has something in their hand. What is it? Draw something in their hand. (Give them some time.) OK, the person is saying something. Write down what the person is saying. (Give some time.) Now, over on the side of the paper, give the person a name and an age, and tell where they live. (Give some time.) Write down where they go to school and what they do in their spare time.

Example 2

Imagine an ideal home visit. What would that be like? We want you to draw your ideal home visit. Draw yourself and your baby. Put a little arrow to the baby and tell us how old the baby is when this ideal visit occurs. (Give some time.) The ideal nurse comes and she brings a gift for you and a gift for the baby. What does she bring? Draw the nurse and draw what she brings for you and the baby. (Give some time.) The nurse has a nametag with the name of her organization on it. What organization is listed on the nametag in this ideal visit? Give her a nametag and list the organization. (Give some time.) The nurse does something while she is there that is really helpful. What does she do? Draw it. (Give some time.) The nurse leaves you with a message that you really wanted or needed to hear. Draw a bubble from her mouth and write down the message she leaves. (Give some time.) Finally, in a corner, jot down three characteristics this ideal home visitor has that are important to you.

Example 3

Draw a picture of an employee of this organization. You don't have to be an artist; a stick figure is just fine. Draw an arrow to his or her mouth and write down what they say to their supervisor about the organization. Draw an arrow to the head and write down what he or she thinks about the organization. Then draw an arrow to the heart and write down what he or she feels about the organization. (We draw an example of the picture and have people copy the picture and fill in the blanks. We don't give examples of what they say, think or feel because we don't want to lead or bias people.)

As with all these participatory exercises, the benefit is in the discussion following the picture drawing. The picture is merely the stimulus that helps participants collect their thoughts and explain how they see a concept or idea. However, the pictures can be incredibly helpful in sharing the focus group findings with others. We often include a few of these pictures in the final report.

Using Your Imagination

Occasionally moderators will ask participants to imagine or dream about how things could be different. The challenge for the moderator is to establish the timing of the experience so that participants are ready for the exercise. For example, after participants have talked about the pros and cons of an alternative, the moderator might tell participants that there is a magic wand, hat, or device that allows them to make their dream come true. The moderator passes around the wand or hat, and as each participant holds the wand or puts on the hat, he or she also shares his or her dream. Or, participants might be asked to close their eyes and imagine that they are on a special journey in a faraway land. Along the way, they discover a special box that holds answers to great problems and difficulties that people have. When you open the box, you find the answer to the problem. What is in the box?

The moderator begins the experience by changing the pace of the group discussion. Up to this point, participants were answering questions and conversing with others. Now, the moderator changes the mood of the conversation, perhaps by asking for a moment of silence, by using music to create a period of relaxation, or by guided imagery. This question often works well because it is different from what participants expect. The request seems unusual, unexpected, and sometimes even goofy. If you decide to use it, plan carefully for how you introduce the question.

Developing a Campaign

Recently, several youth focus group studies have used a "campaign" questioning strategy. The session begins with the moderator asking questions of the youth about campaigns. "What is a campaign?" "Tell us about where you've seen campaigns." "What happens in a campaign?" "What are the things that make up a campaign?" During this first part, the young people typically talk about political campaigns and sometimes campaigns for schools, teams, or local causes. Campaigns have slogans, speakers, banners, songs, balloons, and celebrities. The

EXAMPLE

Imagination Questions

Here are three examples of questions asking participants to use their imagination.

Example 1

A moderator was seeking creative suggestions for developing an educational event for food service workers. Designers had come up with the theme of having a carnival. She asked participants to close their eyes, listen to carnival music, and imagine themselves at the carnival. They were led through a guided imagery and asked to jot down notes or try to remember what came to mind for each question. The group participants (who were helping design the carnival) were asked to:

Imagine promotional materials for the carnival that got you excited to go. How did they get your attention? What did they say? What did they look like?

Imagine arriving at the carnival. What do you hear? What do you see? What do you smell?

Imagine walking around the carnival and being excited about certain exhibits. What do the exhibits look like? What are they about? What are people doing?

Imagine going back to school and telling coworkers that the event was great and incredibly useful. What made it great? What made it useful?

After they had been guided through the exercise, the moderator asked each question again, and asked participants to share what they had imagined for each step.

Example 2

An organization was exploring solutions to employees' child care problems. The moderator said: "Here is a magic wand. I'll pass it around the table and when you receive it, give your magical solution to the problem. By waving the wand, your solution will come true. Take the wand and tell us your solution."

Example 3

Yet, other studies have asked people to imagine ideal futures: "Close your eyes for a moment. Imagine that you have been cryogenically frozen and you wake up twenty years in the future. You are completely OK, and you awake to an ideal world. What is the university like in this ideal world?"

moderator then asks the participants to develop a campaign that will get other young people to do something—perhaps eat more fruits and vegetables, get more exercise, or avoid drugs and alcohol. The campaign is aimed at other kids. Those in the focus group plan the strategy, complete with slogans, speakers, music, or whatever they think is needed to be effective. There is a supply of materials, such as markers and colored paper, for the kids to use in developing their campaign. The group can be divided into two groups of three to five participants to work for forty-five minutes to an hour and then reassemble. Kids then share their campaigns and talk about what they like best about each campaign.

This strategy works well with youth because it allows them to be active, to use their expertise, and to have fun. You can get creative with this. One researcher provided T-shirts and caps to the kids, so they could identify themselves as their own marketing group. The researcher gets ideas and learns which strategies the target audience finds effective. This campaign strategy also works with adults in promoting social issues, community activities, wellness campaigns, and a host of other efforts.

Doing Something Before the Focus Group

Sometimes focus group participants are asked to do a task before coming to the focus group. The task helps the participant prepare for the group discussion. This task could consist of visiting a location, reviewing materials or a Web site, keeping a log of activities, or taking

EXAMPLE

Doing Something Before the Group

Example 1

In a study of mosquito control, focus group participants were asked to keep a fourteen-day log of their experiences with mosquitoes. The forms for the log were sent to participants in advance. Participants were paid to complete the log and attend the focus group. The logs helped participants recall their experiences in the previous two-week period and the researchers collected the documents for later content analysis.

Example 2

In a study of women's attitudes toward car repair, the researcher sent each participant a disposable camera and a scrapbook two weeks prior to the group. Each page of the scrapbook had a caption, like "Take a picture of your car." "Take a picture of where you take your car to get it fixed." "Take a picture of how you feel when your car breaks down." "Take a picture of how you feel while you car is being repaired." Participants were asked to take a picture for each caption, have the film developed, put the pictures in the scrapbook, and bring the completed scrapbook to the focus group. Participants were asked to share their pictures in the group. The client collected all the scrapbooks. Participants were paid $100 to develop the scrapbook and participate in the focus group.

photographs of the topic of interest or any activity that provides experience with the research topic.

The Process We Use to Develop a Questioning Route

So how does one go about developing a questioning route for a focus group study? Here is a process that works well for us. Typically we do the following:

1. Brainstorming
2. Phrasing the questions
3. Sequencing the questions
4. Estimating time for questions
5. Getting feedback from others
6. Testing the questions

Step 1. Brainstorming

We invite a few people who are familiar with the purpose of the study to meet to brainstorm questions. We look for people with different backgrounds: expertise in the topic, knowledge of the organization requesting the study, experience with focus groups, and familiarity with the focus group participants. Usually the team includes us, the client, and others whom the client invites. Often we plan for four to six people and a one- to two-hour meeting. We begin by reviewing the purpose of the study and the intended audiences, and then we ask people to throw out ideas for questions that should be asked. One person records all the ideas. People are allowed to comment on questions as they come up, but we try not to get stuck talking about one question. Sometimes the ideas for questions dry up quickly. Then we will ask for ideas in different ways: What would you like to know after we are done? What kind of decision do you want to make? What kind of information would be helpful to you? At this point, we are looking for key questions—those questions that will drive the study. We don't worry too much about the other kinds of questions. After an hour or two, we typically have plenty of questions to begin the next step.

A group is great for generating ideas for questions, but a group isn't efficient for refining the questions. Therefore, we adjourn our brainstorming meeting, and then one or two people take responsibility for the next step—phrasing and sequencing the questions.

TIP

Selecting Useful Questions

After a brainstorming session, we have many more questions than could actually fit in a questioning route. Where do we start? Which ones do we include? It helps to have mental screens for the questions, like these:

Is this a "nice-to-know" or a "need-to-know" question? Nice-to-know questions often arise from curiosity but aren't crucial to the study. Need-to-know questions arise out of a need

for information. We include need-to-know questions first.

A variation of the question above is, What would you do with this information if you had it? Is it going to help you move closer to your goal? We sometimes ask clients these questions to help us understand what would be useful to them. We start with questions with the most potential to provide useful information.

Step 2. *Phrasing the Questions*

Phrasing and sequencing really happen at the same time. The researcher examines the list of questions and begins by pulling those questions that seem key to the study and editing them (phrasing them) so they will work in a focus group (e.g., take out jargon, make them open-ended). Then, as the researcher pulls additional questions, he or she begins to build the questioning route. Let's consider the strategies for phrasing questions.

Use Open-Ended Questions

Open-ended questions allow the respondents to determine the direction of the response. The answer is not implied, and the type or manner of response is not suggested. Individuals are encouraged to respond based on their specific situation. The major advantage of the open-ended question is that it reveals what is on the interviewee's mind as opposed to what the interviewer suspects is on the interviewee's mind. For example, consider these open-ended questions: "What did you think of the program?" "How did you feel about the conference?" "Where do you get new information?" "What do you like best about the proposed program?" "What do you like least about the proposed program?"

Some questions are deceptive and appear to be open-ended but are really closed-ended questions in disguise. Questions that include phrases such as "how satisfied," "to what extent," or "how much" imply answers that fall within a specified range, such as very satisfied, to a great extent, or a great deal. Compare the questions "How satisfied were you with the services you received?" and "How did you feel about the services you received?" The more open-ended question begs for more description, more explanation.

Closed-ended questions aren't totally off-limits. They can provide very helpful information. You may want some very simple information, such as asking kids in a study of school lunch, "How many of you usually bring a bag lunch?" Or, toward the end of the group interview, it may be productive to narrow the types of responses and bring greater focus to the answers by shifting to closed-ended questions. Also, bounding the questions may be helpful to a moderator trying to regain control of a rambling discussion or in situations when the topic requires more specific insights. For example, the moderator might say, "Which of these three options do you like best?"

Ask Participants to Think Back

The "think-back" question asks participants to reflect on their personal experiences and then respond to a specific question. "Think back to when you began working at the public health service. What attracted you to the position?" Or, "Think back to the last time you registered for a course at the university. What was that experience like?" The "think-back" phrase helps establish a context for the response. These words let participants know that you want them to be specific and grounded in their experiences as opposed to "hearsay" from others or just repeating community beliefs and values. People often give great examples of their experiences.

There's a tendency for participants to respond to the more immediate interviewing experience—the here and now—unless you ask them to shift themselves to another timeframe. This focus on the past increases the reliability of the responses because it asks about specific experiences as opposed to current intentions or future possibilities. The question asks what the person has done as opposed to what might be done in the future. The shift is from what might be, or ought to be, to what has been. This time shift cues the respondent to speak from experience as opposed to wishes and intentions.

Avoid Asking Why

The "why" question has sharpness or pointedness to it that reminds one of interrogations. The respondent tends to feel confronted and defensive. Also, "why" questions imply a rational answer. Unfortunately, these "why" questions present problems because in real life, people make decisions based on impulse, habit, tradition, or other nonrational processes. When asked why, respondents feel like they should have a rational answer appropriate to the situation. The participant "intellectualizes" the answer and speaks from the brain and not from deeper forces that motivate behavior.

If the researcher decides to use a "why" question, it should be specific. Paul Lazarfeld (1934/1986) has called this the principle of specification. Lazarfeld's principle of specification is that "why" questions are answered in two ways. When asked why, the respondent may respond on (a) the basis of "influences" that prompted the action or (b) the basis of certain desirable "attributes." "Why" questions can be messy to analyze if participants aren't clear whether you are asking for influences or attributes.

Let's use Lazarfeld's model to examine the responses to a seemingly simple question: "Why did you go to the zoo?"

> Influence answer: "Because my kids really wanted to go."
>
> Attribute answer: "Because I wanted to see the Beluga whale."

What seems like a straightforward and simple question can really be answered on several dimensions. The first answer describes an influence, and the second answer relates to a feature or attribute of the zoo. The preferred strategy is to break the "why" question down into different questions. For example:

> Influence: "What prompted (influenced, caused, made) you to go to the zoo?" Or,
>
> Attribute: "What features of the zoo do you particularly like?"

A less direct approach is to ask people "what" or "how" they feel about the object of discussion. Often people can describe the feelings they had when they considered using a particular product or program. In addition, they can probably describe the anticipated consequences from using the product or program.

Keep Questions Simple

Beginning researchers tend to make focus group questions too complex. Simple, clear questions are essential. For example, don't ask, "What are the ingredients that are associated with healthy living?" Instead, ask, "Describe a healthy lifestyle." Think of the shortest way to ask the question clearly. The best focus group questions are stated simply. When these questions are asked, the participants immediately

CAUTION

The Limit of Think-Back Questions

"Think-back" questions should be limited to events or experiences that are fairly recent or particularly memorable. If the participants can't readily remember the experience, the question won't work.

know what is asked for, and within seconds they are on their way to providing an answer. By contrast, avoid questions that have multiple interpretations. The participant hesitates because the question is confusing. Then, while thinking, he or she becomes distracted by the comments of other participants and forgets his or her train of thought.

Simple questions do not yield simple answers! It is often the simple question that gets the participant to bring shape and form to the discussion. It pulls out assumptions and lays bare the core principles. You can spot the simple questions because they typically have few words, no jargon or insider language, and no commas, semicolons, or hyphens. The simple question is not condescending or childish. It's a sophisticated question that gets at the core of the topic.

Perhaps the most distinctive feature of simple questions is that they are memorable. Too often, participants forget the question, in part because it is too complex. The memorable question is one that continues to "ring" in their heads. Even if one participant gets off topic, another participant remembers the question and brings the discussion back on track.

Make questions sound conversational, and use words the people in the group would use.

Sometimes we get caught up in our own jargon or the language of our profession. This doesn't work well in focus groups. Insider language is offensive and doesn't communicate well to outsiders. We always try to ask questions in a way that sounds conversational. And we try to use language that is comfortable for the types of people we are asking. If we are talking with special education teachers, we may use more technical language than if we are talking with parents or students. If we are working with health care providers, we may use more technical language than if we are talking to patients or their family members. Sometimes we imagine, OK, if I were in the backyard talking to the neighbors, how would I ask this? We don't use acronyms unless they are well known or we

TIP

Make Complex Questions Visual

If you have a question that is difficult to put into few words, write it on a flip chart before the group begins and flip to it when you get to that question in the discussion. The visual cue helps people understand and remember the complex question.

explain them. Our goal is not to baffle them with our vocabulary or puff up our egos but to seek to be enlightened by them.

Be Cautious About Giving Examples

Examples are like mental ruts. Although they provide ideas for the type of response, they also limit the thinking of respondents. Suppose you are doing a study of customer satisfaction, and because the topic is broad, you decide to use the example of how complaints are handled. Well, handling complaints is only one facet of customer satisfaction, and because it evokes memories and vivid experiences, it can dominate the conversation and prevent other dimensions from emerging. If you do give examples, give them as probes after participants have already given their insights.

Step 3. Sequencing the Questions

Now, let's think about the sequence of the questions. Focus group questions are not just thrown together. The researcher arranges the questions with care. This question sequence is the reason we use the word *focus* in the name. This focused sequence is sensible to participants. It provides an opportunity for participants to anchor their opinions and then build on those views. Here is how we sequence:

General Before Specific

The most common procedure in arranging questions is to go from general to specific—that is, begin with general overview questions that lead to more specific questions of critical interest. Avoid presenting participants with key questions without first establishing the context created by more general questions. For example, suppose a series of focus group interviews will be held with young people. The purpose is to learn their perceptions of youth organizations and eventually to identify an effective means of advertising a particular organization. It would be premature to begin with questions on advertising the organization. Instead, the moderator might ask the participants to describe their favorite youth organization or to describe what they like about youth clubs. Later in the discussion, the moderator might narrow the topic to focus on a specific youth organization under investigation. Perhaps toward the end of the discussion, the moderator might solicit opinions on several different approaches that are being considered for advertising the youth group.

EXAMPLE

Moving From General to Specific Questions

An actual illustration of the general to specific technique of focusing questions comes from Hawaii. To gain insights into how consumers use Kona coffee, the moderator began with questions about gourmet foods, then asked about gourmet beverages. When a participant suggested Kona coffee, the moderator then encouraged discussion of how and when this type of coffee was used.

The funnel analogy is helpful because it presents the researcher with a visual guide for arranging questions. The funneling concept is used to move the discussion from broad to narrow, from general to specific, or from abstract to specific. The funneling begins with fairly broad discussion and is followed by a series of narrower, more focused questions. Just how broad should the beginning questions be? Part of that depends on the number of questions you have and the amount of time scheduled for the focus group.

Positive Questions Before Negative Ones

If you want to ask a negative question, first ask the question phrased in a positive way. For example, if you want to ask, "What don't you like about eating in the cafeteria?" first ask, "What do you like about eating in the cafeteria?" Give participants the chance to comment on both positive and negative experiences or observations. This strategy usually works better when the first request is for positive items. Perhaps it was our mothers' exhortations that we shouldn't say something bad unless we've first said something good.

The benefit of using both positive and negative questions is that it allows participants to comment on both sides of the issue, and in some situations, this is particularly important. At times, focus group participants get in a rut and become excessively critical. It's reasonable for employees of an organization, students in an educational setting, or military personnel to launch into criticism of those who have control and power. In situations when participants begin with negative features

and tend to dwell on the undesirable factors, there is value in "turning the tables" and asking for opposite views. "So what are the benefits of working around here?" "What's positive about being a student here?" and so on.

Often the transition from positive to negative aspects is smooth and comfortable, but care is needed so that it isn't premature. One rather predictable scenario is that although positive attributes are being discussed, a participant might disagree with the positive statement and want to offer a contrary point of view. This can easily lead into the discussion of negative attributes without further exploration of the positive features. Here the moderator will need to exercise mild control and encourage the group to complete the discussion of the positive attributes before shifting to the less desirable features.

Uncued Questions Before Cued Questions

The rule of thumb is to ask the uncued question first and then follow up with cues to prompt additional discussion. For example, a moderator could ask, "What are the needs in this neighborhood?" as an uncued question. After people discuss this question, the moderator could list categories that help spur additional thoughts (e.g., children, teenagers, young families, older families, the elderly, or safety, health, child care, jobs) and ask, "When you think of these categories, do any other needs come to mind?"

If the researcher is particularly interested in the needs of teenagers but those needs don't come up in the discussion, the researcher has no way of knowing whether needs of teenagers aren't really important in that neighborhood or if they were just overlooked in the discussion. The researcher has to ask. The cues themselves require some thought. They are developed before the focus group. They are limited in number yet also reasonably exhaustive.

When using uncued and cued questions, it may also be helpful to include an "all-things-considered" question, described earlier. In this question, the participants are asked to identify the one factor (need, concern, etc.) that they consider to be the most important (critical, necessary to address, etc.). Responses to this question greatly aid the analysis. An analysis error sometimes made in focus groups is to assume that what is most frequently mentioned is also most important.

Step 4. *Estimating Time for Questions*

Another common error of beginning focus group researchers is to try to ask too many questions. We have seen questioning routes with thirty questions. In a two-hour group, that is less than four minutes per question—too little time to expect in-depth discussion. Researchers tend to get superficial, top-of-the-mind information if they don't allow enough time for discussion.

Focus groups are typically two hours long. Successful groups have been conducted in less time, particularly with children or teenagers or on narrowly focused studies. We also occasionally hear of focus groups lasting more than two hours. The two-hour time limit, however, is a physical and psychological limit for most people. Don't go beyond the two-hour maximum unless there is a special event or circumstance that makes it comfortable for participants, such as providing lunch or dinner.

Once we have a draft-questioning route, we estimate how much time we should spend on each question, typically five, ten, fifteen, or twenty minutes. When planning a two-hour group, we allow a little flexible time at the front end, about fifteen minutes. If everyone is there on time, we start right away. But occasionally, we will have to wait until enough people arrive to begin the group. We wait about fifteen minutes and then begin with whoever is there. We also allow time at the end of the group for ending questions and summarizing (at least fifteen minutes). This leaves about ninety minutes for the opening, introductory, transition, and key questions. We add up the time we have assigned the questions and decide if we need to add or delete questions.

When estimating time for the questions, consider the following:

- *The complexity of the question.* Some questions can be answered in a matter of seconds. For example, we occasionally ask very simple questions such as, "How many of you usually eat school lunch? Raise your hand if you usually eat school lunch." Other questions demand more time and discussion, such as, "What do you think of the school cafeteria?"

- *The category of questions.* Opening and introductory questions typically don't take much time. Allow the most time for key questions.

- *The level of participants' expertise.* A group of experts will have more to say than a group of nonexperts on any topic. So experts need more time per question. One way to deal with this is to limit the number of questions to be asked of experts. For example, we may include fourteen questions in a discussion with nonusers of a program but include only ten questions in the questioning route for users of the program.

- *The size of the focus group.* A group of nine participants will usually discuss each question longer than a group of six participants.
- *The level of discussion you want related to the question.* If you don't want in-depth information about a particular question, allow less time for it. If you want in-depth data or insights, allow enough time for participants to wrestle with the question.

Step 5. *Getting Feedback From Others*

Once the questioning route is completed, it is time to send it back to the team that brainstormed the questions for their review. Usually it isn't necessary to physically get back together to review the questions. Often, e-mail or fax works well for getting the draft-questioning route back to people. Ask people to think about the following:

- Are these the right questions? Will they get the type of information you need?
- Do you understand the questions? Are any of them confusing to you?
- Do the questions seem to flow from one topic to another?
- Are these the words that people in the groups would use to talk about the issue?
- What have we missed?

It is not unusual to run through several drafts before the team feels comfortable with the questions. If you get to a point when people start to nitpick, it is definitely time to pilot test the questions.

Step 6. *Testing the Questions*

Before using the questions in a group, we test them. Sometimes it is as simple as finding a few people who fit the focus group screen and asking them the questions. At this point, we ask the questions as if we were conducting an individual interview. We pay attention to two things:

- How easy it is to ask the question? Do the words flow smoothly, or do we stumble when we ask it? A question that seemed simple when we wrote it on the page may be awkward

TIP

Put the Date on Each Draft to Minimize Confusion

With multiple revisions, it is easy to get confused about which draft is the latest. Using different colored paper and numbering the draft versions are helpful, but it also helps to date each draft.

when we ask it aloud. If we stumble, we rephrase it to make it easier to say—more conversational.

- Does the question seem confusing to the participants? Do they hesitate too long? Do they look confused? Do they give an answer that shows the question is confusing? Do they ask for clarification? If so, we ask them to tell us about what is confusing and ask for their help in making the question simpler.

After we have tested the questions with a few people, we hold the first focus group. We don't pilot test the questions in the group. It is so time and labor intensive to set up a group that we want to be able to use the results from the discussion, rather than consider it a pilot. If a question doesn't work in the first group, we revise it before the second group. At the end of the first group, we may ask the participants to help us revise a question that seemed awkward or confusing.

Changing Questions: The Importance of Consistency

Remember, if you wish to compare and contrast responses across groups, you must keep the questions consistent. If you change questions from group to group, you lose your ability to compare. The general rule is to maintain as much consistency as possible throughout the series of focus groups because it is in comparison and contrast that themes and patterns emerge from the data. Information obtained from a single focus group can yield interesting and, at times, helpful insights, but the researcher just doesn't know if similar findings would occur in another group. In analysis, the researcher strives for theoretical saturation that is possible only with consistent questioning.

But what about studies in which you have several different types of participants—groups of parents, students, teachers, and food service workers? Should you use the same questioning route for all groups? If you want to compare how teachers, students, and parents see or feel about a particular topic, you must have a core set of questions that remains consistent across groups. Often, most of the key questions will stay the same so you can compare and contrast how different types of participants answer the question. However, you may want to ask some questions that tap into the expertise or experience unique to a particular group. For example, in a study of how to increase kids' consumption of fruits and vegetables while at school, we asked the food service

BACKGROUND

Circumstances When Questions Might Change

Occasionally it is wise to change or eliminate a question in a focus group interview. Here are two circumstances when it should be considered.

1. Change the question if it clearly doesn't work. This is often spotted in one of the first focus groups. Here are three signals that a question doesn't work:

(a) when there is silence and participants look baffled; (b) when participants tell you that they don't understand the question; and (c) when participants talk, but aren't answering the question.

2. Change the question if saturation has clearly occurred and the responses are of limited use. In many studies, theoretical saturation occurs somewhere between three and twelve focus groups. When conducting a sizable number of focus groups, such as more than twelve, there is little to gain by continuing to ask questions of the same type of participants when the responses are predictable and of limited use. There is considerably more to gain by changing questions to build on what you have learned in the earlier groups. Based on what we have heard in the early groups, we may adapt the question to move it to another level.

workers, "What makes it tough to serve fruits and vegetables at school?" This is an important question that highlights barriers for food service personnel, and they have unique expertise to answer this question. However, it wouldn't make sense to ask the other groups this question.

SUMMARY

Too often, questions are hastily put together because they "sound good" to the researchers. Poor questions are confusing to participants and are virtually impossible to analyze. In this chapter, we've highlighted the qualities that result in good questioning routes. These questions are conversational, clear, and short—among other things. Not all questions are alike, and five distinct types of questions were discussed: opening, introductory, transition, key, and ending questions. We shared some questions that ask participants to go beyond the sit-and-talk response. Finally, we shared a process for developing questions.

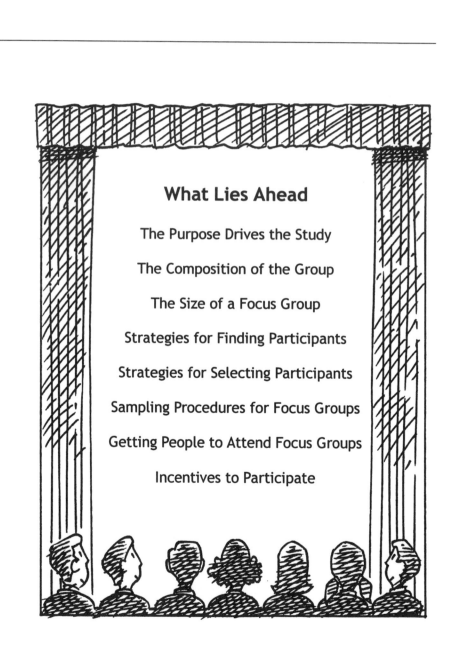

What Lies Ahead

The Purpose Drives the Study

The Composition of the Group

The Size of a Focus Group

Strategies for Finding Participants

Strategies for Selecting Participants

Sampling Procedures for Focus Groups

Getting People to Attend Focus Groups

Incentives to Participate

4

Participants in a Focus Group

Who should be invited? How many people should participate? How should participants be identified? What does it take to get people to attend? How many groups should be conducted?

Too often, public-sector organizations underestimate the importance of careful recruitment of participants. Market research firms place huge emphasis and spend huge amounts of money on recruiting. Public and nonprofit organizations operate within a different environment. Most can't spend huge amounts of money on recruiting. They operate under different traditions, constraints, rules, and procedures.

Successful recruitment may not require huge sums of money, but it does require special effort. Sure, nonprofit employees are always inviting people to participate in meetings and events through conventional methods such as newsletters, form letter invitations, or announcements at meetings. These don't work well for focus groups. If the organization is truly interested in getting quality information, then these methods should be set aside because they will not be effective in getting the right number of the right people to attend. Instead, substitute a systematic and deliberate process.

Also, employees in public organizations may feel that their traditions and values require them to conduct meetings open to the public. In some instances, decision makers may want to allow anyone and everyone to participate in the focus groups. These sessions resemble public hearings in which citizens come to ventilate or to watch others as they share their wrath. Focus groups are not open public meetings because this defeats critical characteristics that are essential for the focus group to work, such as having homogeneous participants, a permissive environment, and a limited number of people.

To illustrate the difficulties that can occur, consider the story of a suburban community. The city council wanted to build a new fire

CAUTION

Nonprofit Organizations Often Have Difficulty Recruiting

Nonprofit organizations that do their own focus group recruiting often have difficulty because they assume focus group participants are like volunteers. However, the motivation of volunteers may be quite different from that of focus group participants. Volunteers are already committed to the organization. They give their time and talents freely. Think about people who aren't committed to the organization, and think about what it would take to get them to participate. Think about what would keep them from participating.

station. The old station needed major improvements. It would cost more to repair the old building than to build a new station, but the city needed to pass a bond issue to build the new station, a tough task. Twice before, the city council had placed the bond issue on the ballot, and twice the referendum was defeated. To avoid an embarrassing third defeat, the officials commissioned a research firm to study the possibility of a favorable vote. The research firm conducted "focus groups" within the municipality. The public was invited to attend any or all of the discussions held in various places in the community. Announcements were made on cable TV, posters were placed in public buildings and on bulletin boards in grocery stores and pharmacies, and special ads were placed in newspapers. Naturally, the attendance varied, and the discussions were more like town meetings. The research firm's findings indicated that the vote would now be favorable, and the city council decided to move ahead with the election. The election results were a huge disappointment to the elected officials. The bonding bill was resoundingly defeated. In hindsight, the city council discovered that the opponents to the fire stations were largely senior citizens who were quite concerned about increased property taxes. Seniors didn't attend the open meetings, but they did vote!

Those who supported building a new fire station showed up at the focus groups. Residents who were against the new station just ignored the meetings but showed up for the election. In this situation, the lack of careful procedures for selecting respondents produced embarrassing and erroneous results. Also, generalizations or projections to a population based on limited focus group interviews are risky.

The Purpose Drives the Study

To decide who should be invited to the group interview, think back to the purpose of the study. Usually the purpose is to describe how certain people feel or think about something—people who have certain things in common. What kind of people are you interested in? What kind of people can give you the information you are looking for? The purpose should guide the invitation decision. The statement of purpose may require refinement to ensure that the target audience has the degree of specification needed for the study. For example, the researcher might have initially identified community residents as the target audience but later, after some thought, restricted the audience to unmarried residents between the ages of eighteen and forty. In other situations, participants might be identified in broad terms such as homemakers, teenagers, or residents of a geographic area.

The purpose of the study is the first of three ingredients that influence the decision of whom to invite. The second includes everything you currently know about your target audience and groups that are close to your target. Is the target audience distinctive, identifiable, and reasonable to locate? In focus groups, the goal is to have a homogeneous audience. There are no precise rules that determine homogeneity, but rather, it is a judgment call based on your knowledge about the audience and the situation.

Third, the budget influences the degree of specification. Simply put, how many different groups can you afford to conduct? Or another way of asking the question is, How much are you willing to invest in this study? If resources are scarce and only three focus groups can be conducted, you will need to decide what type of people will give you the most meaningful information.

Let's suppose that a religious group decides to use focus groups to discover what would prompt new people to attend services. The religious group would need to decide what type of members it wants to attract—teenagers, young families, single-parent families, seniors, residents living within a geographic area, and so on. If several different audiences are sought, then it is advisable to conduct a series of focus groups with each audience category: teens, single-parent families, and so on. A decision is needed regarding the research budget. What is this information worth? With X resources, one audience category might be investigated, but 2X resources are needed to include two audiences, 3X for three audiences, and so on. The research budget should include the actual costs of conducting the focus groups and the volunteer time needed to conduct the study.

The Composition of the Group

The focus group is characterized by homogeneity but with sufficient variation among participants to allow for contrasting opinions. By homogeneity, we mean participants have something in common that you are interested in, such as the following:

- *An occupation.* (You want to explore professional development needs of practicing dentists in the state.)
- *Past use of a program or service.* (You want to evaluate an educational program, comparing the experiences of people who completed the program in the past year with groups of people who dropped out of the program.)
- *Age.* (You want to talk to teenagers about smoking. You conduct some groups with 7th graders, some with 9th graders, and some with 11th graders.)
- *Gender.* (You want to talk to men who have had false positives on prostate screening tests to find out how this affected their quality of life.)
- *Family characteristics.* (You want to talk to women who have had babies in the past year to get help in designing a program for new moms.)

There are at least two reasons we are concerned about homogeneity. One is for analysis purposes. The other is the participants' comfort—the degree to which sharing will be influenced by differences in participants' characteristics.

Think about your analysis when considering group composition. If you want to compare and contrast different types of people's views, you must separate these different types of people into different groups. For example, it is much easier to analyze differences between users and nonusers when they are in separate groups than if they are mixed together. So if you are interested in similarities and differences between or among different types of people, separate them and conduct a series of groups with each type of group.

Related to this, it is a fallacy to assume that any one individual can "represent" his or her neighborhood, race, gender, or culture. Each person speaks for himself or herself. When asked, however, these individuals may attempt to offer insights about the opinions of the entire group, and the degree to which they have similar opinions may vary greatly. If you want to capture the opinions of a certain group of people, then you'll need to conduct a sufficient number of focus groups with that particular category of people. A focus group of diverse people is not sensitive enough to pick up trends of subcategories of people.

The other reason (besides analysis) that we consider homogeneity is the degree to which these factors will influence sharing within the group discussion. We want people to feel comfortable to share. Some mixes of participants do not work well because of limited understanding of other lifestyles and situations. For example, care must be exercised in mixing individuals from different life stages and styles unless the topic clearly cuts across these life stages and styles. Recently, we were conducting focus groups with women who were pregnant. We wanted their help in designing a health and education program for new moms. Our only screens were that they be pregnant and from the participating county. We had teenagers who didn't want to be pregnant in the same groups with forty-year-old women who were ecstatic about being pregnant for the first time. The young women tended to be quiet and deferred to the others in the group. In hindsight, it would have been better if we had held separate groups for the teenage moms. You strive for a balance between having enough variation within the group to get contrast and yet not so much variation that participants are inhibited and defer to those whom they perceive to be more experienced, knowledgeable, or better educated.

At times it is unwise to mix genders in focus groups. Men may have a tendency to speak more frequently and with more authority when in groups with women—sometimes called the "peacock effect"—and this can irritate women in the group.

A related topic is the involvement of both husband and wife in the same focus group discussion. There is a tendency for one spouse to remain silent and defer to the talkative spouse. Even if the silent spouse disagrees, it appears that he or she is reluctant to comment even when such comments are solicited from the moderator. As a result, we have found that focus groups of four married couples turn out to be a discussion of four people with four rather silent partners.

The Size of a Focus Group

The traditionally recommended size of the focus group within marketing research is ten to twelve people. However, when dealing with complex topics or with knowledgeable participants, this size is too large. The ideal size of a focus group for most noncommercial topics is six to eight participants. Don't plan focus groups with more than ten participants because they are difficult to control, and they limit each person's opportunity to share insights and observations. In addition, group dynamics change when participants want to but aren't able to describe their experiences. For example, if people do not have an opportunity to share experiences in the total group, they may lean over to the next person to whisper. This phenomenon is a signal that the group is too large. Small focus groups, or mini-focus groups, with four

TIP

*Ideal Size of
a Focus Group*

The ideal size of a
focus group is usually
from six to eight
participants.

to six participants are becoming increasingly popular because the smaller groups are easier to recruit and host, and they are more comfortable for participants. The disadvantage of the mini-focus group is that it limits the total range of experiences simply because the group is smaller. Four people will have had fewer total experiences than a dozen.

Often the questioning route and participant characteristics yield clues as to the ideal size of the groups. If the questions are meant to gain understanding of people's experiences, the researcher typically wants more in-depth insights. This is usually best accomplished with smaller groups. Also, smaller groups are preferable when the participants have a great deal to share about the topic or have had intense or lengthy experiences with the topic of discussion. For example, parents of children in special education programs have a lot to share when talking about special education. They feel strongly about this experience. And they often want to share tips and information with the other participants. Because of their passion and experience, it is wise to plan for smaller groups so everyone has a chance to share. Larger groups (eight people) work well when the questions are meant to pilot test materials or ideas and when the participants don't have a lot of knowledge about the topic. For example, users of a program will have more to say about a program than nonusers will. Therefore, you can recruit larger groups of nonusers than users.

Strategies for Finding Participants

Several strategies are used to identify participants for focus group interviews. These include the following.

The List

If possible, find an existing list of people fitting your screens. A list is fast and economical. This could include existing lists of clients, members, employees, or those who use services of the organization. If it is needed, try to get more than the name, phone number, and address. The organization may have a database of customers' sociodemographic characteristics or employees with years of experience, age, and educational level. These additional demographics may be of use in screening participants. Make sure the list is up-to-date. Some lists are well maintained, but others contain substantial errors.

Once the characteristics for selection have been determined, the researcher might contact existing groups in the community to find if they have members with these characteristics. Are there churches, recreational groups, or community groups that might have members like the people you are seeking? Some groups will be reluctant to release names or have restrictions on releasing member lists. Organizations are more cooperative when the researcher explains the study and how the participants, the organization, or the community will benefit from the study. Explain that there is no selling, that volunteers can decline to participate, and that participants will receive something for their time. In some situations in the nonprofit environment, a contribution to the group's treasury, tactfully offered, can be a reflection of the value placed on assistance in obtaining names of potential focus group participants.

Piggyback Focus Groups

Piggyback focus groups are added to another event, meeting, or occasion. The participants are gathered for another purpose, and the focus group is held during free time, during a meal, or after hours so as not to interrupt the primary purpose of the gathering. This strategy works well with professional associations or special interest associations, especially when national representation is desired. For example, if you want to conduct focus groups with school principals from around the state, find out when principals get together for regional or statewide meetings. Then arrange to conduct the focus groups while the principals are at the meetings.

On Location

Increasingly, focus groups are being held on location—at the place where the participants come for recreation, shopping, or other purposes. Recruiters stop participants as they pass through a gate, turnstile, hallway, and so on; ask several screening questions; and then offer an invitation to the focus group. The focus group is then held soon after recruitment in a convenient location. Care must be exercised in using this method so that those selected have the requisite characteristics of your target audience. This is the method of choice when the purpose of the study relates to their attendance. Some nonprofit organizations are able to recruit "on location" by inviting people using the services to participate in a discussion. For example, a nature center, zoo, or recreational center might intercept a random assortment of people passing through the gate and invite them to a special discussion. The incentive for participation might be free tickets for another visit.

Recently, a state department of natural resources wanted to learn more about visitors' experiences at state parks. Park employees were trained to conduct focus groups with park visitors. At designated times when a vehicle entered the park, a park employee offered a special invitation. "We'd like to invite one adult from your party to join us for an hour discussion at 7:00 p.m. tonight. We will be talking about the park, and we would like your suggestions. If someone is willing to join our discussion, we'll give you a free bundle of firewood."

Nominations

An effective strategy in community studies is to ask neutral parties for names. These neutral parties are often people who have an opportunity to get to know a number of other people. They might be local merchants, clergy, or influentials, or they might be local residents selected at random. The first step is to identify the specifications for participants in observable terms and then use multiple sources for a nomination list. Only a few names are sought from each source to ensure an adequate mix of participants. Names are then randomly selected from this nomination list for the invitation to the focus group. For example, if you wanted to find senior citizens who live within a community and who own cars, you might seek nominations from local service stations, other senior citizens, or merchants who do business with seniors. If you wanted to find parents from the community who have at least one child in high school but can't get a list from the school, you might ask park and recreation staff, clergy, or perhaps randomly selected teens. In these studies, it is often advantageous to have the identification of focus group participants conducted by local residents who are trusted and have roots in the community. When asking for nominations, make sure to briefly describe how the results of the study will benefit the participants or the community.

A variation of the nomination process is the snowball sample. In a snowball sample, you ask those who have already passed through the selection screen for nominations. The logic is that people know people like themselves. The study must have obvious benefit to the community or individual, or another type of incentive to participation must be used. This snowball sampling could be used at two different times. When making initial contact with the potential participants, you might ask if they know of others who meet the qualifications, or you might ask at the conclusion of the focus group.

Screening/Selection Services

These services are located in most metropolitan areas around the country and are used by commercial market research firms. These agencies have a database of potential focus group participants categorized by sociodemographic characteristics. In addition, they supplement their existing lists with telephone screening if needed. These agencies are listed in the "market research" section of the telephone book. Screening and selection services can be expensive.

Random Telephone Screening

Commercial market research firms also use random telephone screening. The procedure typically begins by random selection of names from a telephone directory. A series of screening questions is used to determine if those called meet the criteria established for the focus group.

Telephone screening is most efficient when searching for participants with fairly common characteristics. As the number of screens increases, the efficiency of this procedure will decrease. For example, in an effort to reach women working outside the home, it was necessary to call fifty households to identify twenty-five women working outside the home. However, only ten were able and willing to participate in a focus group interview at the designated time. If the screen had been more restrictive—for example, women working outside the home with children between the ages of five and ten—then the efficiency of the calling would decrease.

The efficiency of the telephone screening procedures is also affected by the skills of the interviewer. Friendly and sincere calls that convey interest and enthusiasm are most effective. Several years ago, we had an opportunity to work cooperatively with a market research company in helping a community nonprofit organization. The nonprofit organization had employed several college students and used a predetermined interviewing script for calling. The students were finding that people did pass through the screens but then often declined the invitation to attend the discussion. The percentage of invitations accepted dramatically increased when a professional moderator began making the phone calls. The professional conveyed a sense of confidence, friendliness, and sincerity that was developed through years of experience. Because invitations over the phone are often regarded with suspicion, those making the invitations require considerable communication skills.

Ads or Announcements in Newspapers and Bulletin Boards

A recruitment strategy that is used by some marketing agencies is the media ad. For example, "Bought a new car lately? If so, call Ruby at 765-4321." Or an ad placed on the apartment bulletin board: "Wanted, apartment residents who recycle cans, glass, and paper to participate in a market research study. No sales. $25 if you qualify. Call Cynthia McArthur at 876-5432 for more information."

These ads can be effective in certain situations, but the primary draw is often the financial incentive for participation. As a result, there is a slight risk that those motivated by the $25 incentive are different in some way from those who do not call.

The process of identification and recruitment for focus groups is considerably easier when you have names, phone numbers, and background information about these potential participants. Existing directories, membership lists, or organizational records can help identify potential candidates. If you don't have a list, recruiting may take more time and effort.

Strategies for Selecting Participants

We will begin with some rules of thumb that guide the selection of participants for focus group interviews. These rules are then woven into several strategies for identifying participants. First, we offer these general rules to guide the selection process.

Set Exact Specifications— The Screens

As precisely as possible, identify the demographic and observable characteristics of the people you want in the group. These characteristics are called the "screens." Here is an example of screens: A participant must be a woman (Screen 1) from Dakota County (Screen 2) with a baby under the age of 1 (Screen 3) and who is a first-time mom (Screen 4). Be cautious when making selections on nonobservable factors such as attitudes, opinions, or values. Use nonobservable factors only if you have nonbiased empirical data with which to make your decisions.

Maintain Control of Selection Process

The researcher should maintain control of the selection process. At times, it is advisable or even necessary to let others make decisions on the selection process or to carry out strategies used for selection. When others are doing the recruiting, they should fully understand the purpose of the study and the strategy they should use for selecting and recruiting participants. Give precise directions. For example, suppose the Postal Service wants to conduct focus groups with experienced mail sorters and clerks in five major cities. Line supervisors will need to be consulted because of the impact on work floor productivity when workers are absent. These supervisors must be aware of and approve the release of the employees. Because of budget limitations, the researcher may not be able to make advance site visits to conduct the employee screening and make final decisions about participation. In these cases, the researcher will need to depend on the local site supervisors to ensure that a sufficient number of participants are correctly screened and able to leave the work floor during the focus group interview. Unless precise instructions are developed for selection and recruitment, there is a risk that those attending will not be typical of the employee category.

Use the Resources of the Sponsoring Organization in Recruiting

A strategy that has been beneficial in public and nonprofit organizations is to use the skills and strengths of the organization to recruit participants, using carefully laid-out protocol developed by the researcher. Suppose a college wanted to conduct focus groups with alumni to discover the ways alumni preferred to be informed about developments at the school. Also suppose that the budget is tight and the college could conduct focus groups with additional categories of alumni if the alumni office could conduct the recruiting. The researcher might want to use the resources of the alumni office—the class lists by year with demographic data to screen the participants, the clerical staff to make the telephone contacts, and the name of the school and the alumni office to establish credibility and legitimacy. Although a research firm could do all of these tasks, the costs would be greater. However, the researcher must be explicit in laying out the steps needed for selection, giving instructions to staff about how to make the telephone request, and preparing the official letter of request.

Beware of Bias

Selection bias can develop in subtle ways and seriously erode the quality of the study. Here are some examples:

- Beware of participants picked by memory. Memory is limited and selective. Those names that can be readily recalled may differ in substantial ways from the available study population.
- Beware of participants picked because they've expressed concern about the topic. The conscientious supervisor inquires about the purpose of the study, and after it is explained, several names quickly come to mind. These names may include those who have expressed past concern, anger, or frustration with the topic. The supervisor assumes that the study would be improved if it received this input, and also it would show the employees that the supervisor took their concerns seriously enough to suggest they be included in the group discussion.

- Beware of participants picked because they are clones of the supervisor doing the selection. It is a human tendency to believe that those who think like we do are dazzlingly bright. Their logic, vocabulary, and values make sense. The supervisor, with the best of intentions, unwittingly selects those with similar views.

- Beware of participants who are out of the mainstream. In certain situations, the supervisor may not be interested in releasing the most productive employees to attend a focus group. If someone has to go to the focus group interview and the pressure is on the work crew, it's tempting to send the deadwood. Although it may not be your intent, you may have inadvertently assembled the disinterested employees or those who are tuned out to the organization.

Randomly Select From Your Pool

Randomization helps ensure a nonbiased cross section, essentially giving everyone in the pool an equal chance of selection. However, randomization works only if your pool of prospective participants meets your selection criteria. Randomization is rarely done of the entire population but rather of those passing the selection screens. As a result, even though we randomize to limit bias, we may in effect have the wrong screens.

Balance Cost and Quality

Several factors increase recruitment costs: too many selection screens, selection screens based on nonobservable factors, potential participants who are hesitant to participate, studies that aren't explained well, the sponsor's image, interview locations or times that are inconvenient, or when the benefits of participating aren't clear, just to name a few. In virtually all situations, there are multiple options for recruitment—each with differing costs, efficiency, and quality of result. Quality refers to the ability to locate the right people. At times, compromises are needed, such as finding alternative locations or dropping some selection screens. Creative alternatives can sometimes be found through brainstorming.

Nonusers Can Be Difficult to Locate

A number of organizations have tried to get views of nonusers, but some found that recruiting is quite difficult. Typically, there are no reliable lists of nonusers. Even lists of the population are of limited value if the participants are unaware or uncertain of whether they use the product or service. In some ubiquitous services, such as Cooperative Extension, we regularly find that residents do not consider themselves to be users—but in fact, they have made use of information provided by that organization. As a rule of thumb, nonusers are harder to find, often because reliable screening questions are cumbersome, and in some situations, the participant is just not aware of their use.

Users May Differ in Ways That Can Affect the Study

When organizations, either public or private, seek insight from their users, they often discover that these users differ in frequency or intensity of use. Whether your organization provides social services, information, or breakfast cereal, some will use it more often or more in-depth than others. Does this matter for your study? For example, in a study, church members were categorized in two ways: by how frequently they attended church services as well as how much money they contributed annually to the church. Financial contributions are an imprecise measure of intensity, but in this study, the intent was to determine the level of financial support for a new building project— and financial support was essential if the addition was to be feasible.

No Selection Process Is Perfect

We make the best choices we can with the knowledge we have available at the time of the decision. Selection is limited by our human capacities. We may overlook certain aspects of the problem and inadvertently neglect individuals with unique points of view. A test of the selection process is whether you are able to successfully defend the selection process to colleagues and clients. Trade-offs occur constantly and require weighing a possibility of bias or perception of bias against costs.

Sampling Procedures for Focus Groups

When researchers approach focus group interviewing, they carry with them many of the traditions, wisdom, and procedures that were intended for experimental and quantitative studies. Some of these procedures readily transfer; others do not.

Consider random sampling. Most researchers "cut their teeth" on randomization. Because these procedures served them well in some arenas, they may assume that the same procedures are also appropriate for qualitative studies in general and focus group interviews in particular. Randomization essentially removes the bias in selection—that is, all participants possess an equal chance to be involved in the study. Random selection is particularly appropriate when inferences are made to a larger population because of the assumption that opinions, attitudes, or whatever being studied will be normally distributed within that population. Therefore, a random sample of sufficient size will be an adequate substitute for surveying the entire population.

Keep in mind that the intent of focus groups is not to infer but to understand, not to generalize but to determine the range, and not to make statements about the population but to provide insights about how people in the groups perceive a situation. Although a degree of randomization may be used, it is not the primary factor in selection.

When randomization is used in focus groups, it is often for the purpose of eliminating selection bias inherent in some forms of personal recruitment. Typically, lists provide more names than needed, and either a systematic or random sampling procedure should be used in picking the actual names to recruit. In a systematic sample, each *n*th

TIP

Focus Groups Within Organizations

At times, the focus group interview is used with groups that are already established, such as employee work groups, boards of directors, or colleagues. These existing groups may have formal or informal ways of relating to each other that can influence their responses. Superior-subordinate relationships among participants can inhibit discussion. The focus group technique works well when all participants are on an equal basis, but if supervisors, bosses, or even a friend of the boss are in the group, the results might be affected.

Employees might be reluctant to express negative observations in front of coworkers, especially if supervisors are present. Focus groups should be conducted without the presence of supervisors. The key is to help employees feel comfortable. They often want to know who asked for the information, why they asked for it, what decisions will be made with the information, that their comments are confidential, that their names will not be attached to any reports, and who will have access to the audiotapes.

number is picked. For example, if ten names are needed from a list of 200, every twentieth person on the list is selected. A random sample consists of drawing names or ID numbers out of the hat or using a random number table to select from the list of 200 people.

Although the purpose dictates the nature of the selection, practical concerns and credibility temper the process. With all sampling strategies, you must be concerned about the degree to which that strategy could lead to distortions in the data. Anticipate questions about the means of selection and be able to provide the rationale for those decisions.

Getting People to Attend Focus Groups

Some of our first experiences with focus groups were disastrous because so few people showed up. We invited people the same way that we had invited people to other types of meetings, seminars, or workshops. As we analyzed what was wrong, we compared our strategy with the strategies used by market researchers. We discovered our flaws: We were asking people to take a leap of faith and commit time to a topic that seemed insignificant, our invitations weren't personalized, we had no follow-up, we ignored the seasonal time demands on some audiences, we didn't build on existing social and organizational relationships, and we didn't offer incentives. It is surprising that anyone showed up.

Before beginning recruitment, be clear about how you want to describe the study, who is sponsoring the study, and why the study is important. You might want to test this explanation by practicing on colleagues or neighbors or relatives. How does the explanation sound? Honest? Straightforward? Intriguing? Complete enough to make me feel comfortable? Market research firms traditionally don't tell participants who is sponsoring the study. They will describe it as a type or category of product, such as soft drinks, farm pesticides, or automobiles. They avoid naming the specific product so participants will not come with presuppositions. Often the clients want to find out how their product, service, or organization is positioned in relation to the competition. If the participants know the sponsor of the study, they may be biased in their rankings. Market researchers anticipate that people will ask about who is sponsoring the study, and they have a generic response that provides an answer without influencing later responses. At the end of the focus group session, the participants might be provided more specific information on the sponsorship and purpose of the study.

Although it might be acceptable for a private corporation to be coy about sponsorship or purpose, this approach can backfire in the public environment. The public does not respond favorably when a public agency is evasive or appears to be deceptive. In most situations, complete openness is preferred.

Why is this study in the public interest? Who will benefit? What might be done with the results? These are the topics that recruiters need to discuss easily when recruiting participants for public-sector focus groups.

Invitations should be personalized. Each participant should feel that he or she is personally needed and wanted at the interview. Staff members who make telephone invitations should receive special training and practice to extend warm and sincere requests for participants. Invitations that sound like they are being read aren't sincere. The invitation should stress that the potential participant has special experiences or insights that would be of value in the study. Form letters prepared on copy machines are not personal. Individual letters on letterhead stationery that are signed by the moderator should replace them.

Systematic recruitment procedures should be used to provide the necessary follow-up. This involves a series of sequential activities, including the following.

1. Set the Meeting Dates, Times, Locations

The first step is to select meeting dates and times for the group interviews that don't conflict with popular activities or functions. Think about what would be easiest for the participants. Some people have schedules that change on a predictable basis. Farmers, tax consultants, certain small businessmen in rural communities, and teachers are a few examples. Focus groups are best conducted during their slack or off-season. For example, we avoid conducting focus groups with Midwest farmers from mid-April to early August and again from early September to late October. We also avoid dates that conflict with popular sporting events (local or college teams, the World Series, Monday Night Football, etc.); national events (political conventions, elections, etc.); or periods of high television viewing (rating weeks, beginning of fall network shows, etc.).

Give careful thought to the location of your focus group. As we make decisions, we begin by thinking about the participants. We talk to our research colleagues as well as to local experts, influentials, and potential participants. We ask questions, such as the following: Where will participants be comfortable? What is convenient for them? In what types of environments do they normally gather and talk? Does the location present any barriers to communication, such as buildings or rooms that evoke negative reactions or where discussion is inhibited?

Envision the ideal environment from the perspective of the participants. Normally, in real life, where would this conversation take place? Would it be in someone's home? A public place in the community? A local restaurant? In a meeting room at the work site? Around a campfire?

Select a location that is easy to find, safe, and with adequate transportation and parking.

Then consider the research requirements. You will want a location free from visual or audible distractions. Stay away from noisy places. A table is optional but convenient if participants are asked to take notes or make lists. The table is also useful for holding the microphone. Do you need another room for child care? Do you want to use a special room with a one-way mirror to allow for observation? Professional focus group rooms are available in many cities, and the researcher can purchase recruiting services, refreshments, audio or video recording, and a receptionist in addition to the actual room rental. This will severely restrict the possible locations and will increase the costs.

2. Make Personal Contacts With Potential Participants

Once you have set the meeting times, contact potential participants. It is important that this contact be direct and personalized. Usually this first contact is two weeks before the focus group session. If you are contacting professionals or others with busy schedules, you may need to make this contact a month or more in advance.

People are leery of cold calls these days. It helps if you can make a personal connection with the potential participant early in the call, such as the following: "Robert Johnson of Neighborhood Connections said you might be interested in helping us" or "I got your name from Martha Sanford. She is helping us with this project."

People are more likely to take time to attend a focus group interview if they believe the study is important. The sense of importance is

TIP

Make Attending Easy and Attractive

Start by making attendance easy, comfortable, and attractive. Remove barriers that might inhibit participation—child care, transportation, starting time, distance, and so on. What would make it tough for people to participate? What factors would prevent people from attending? Get rid of these. Think about how you can make this easy and attractive.

Hi, Kathy, I got your name from Patty McDuff...

conveyed in several ways. One is by building a convincing case that the study has benefit or value to certain parties. Tell how the results will be used.

Another way to convey importance is through actions. Give thought to who extends the invitation to the focus groups. In the nonprofit and public environment, there is a tendency to have staff or volunteers make the first contact. Too often, these people have a limited understanding of the study, incomplete knowledge of the organization, or little passion for the project. Instead, first, perfect the recruiting strategy yourself and then coach the people who will take on the responsibility. Give them a few talking points. Let them know what should be covered. Don't give them a script to read. You want it to sound conversational, not like the person who calls to sell you siding. Second, avoid the temptation to delegate to the new intern or volunteer and instead seek a "volunteer" from high up in the organization. Look for a person who is recognized, trusted, and respected. If appropriate, ask the chief executive, the block leader, or the head nurse to make initial contacts. You don't want potential participants to feel coerced—like they can't say "no" to this person. But often people feel this study must be really important if this person is taking time to invite them to do this. We have had people tell us it was an honor to be invited by a certain person. Also, participants are more likely to show up if they have said yes to this person they trust and respect. Some people have a gift for getting people to say yes and feeling good about it. Get them to recruit participants.

If the topic or incentive is lackluster or if our past experience with this type of participant dictates it, we sometimes slightly overrecruit, inviting one or two people more than we actually want. Overrecruiting is usually not necessary if the participants see the group as nonthreatening and incentives to participate are good, or if the groups are with employees who will be released from work responsibilities to attend the focus groups.

3. *Send a Personalized Follow-Up Letter*

Just after the participant agrees to be in the focus group, follow up with a personalized letter. For many groups, this is sent one week before the session. The letter is sent on official letterhead with a personal salutation, an inside address, and a signature of someone related to the study (e.g., the moderator, the head of the unit sponsoring the study, the head of the agency sponsoring the study). It provides additional details about the session, location, and topic of discussion. An example of the letter is included in Practice Hint 4.2.

4. *Make a Reminder Phone Contact*

Phone participants the day before the focus group to remind them of the session and confirm their intention to attend. This "dentist"-style phone call serves two purposes. It reinforces the importance of the group ("This must be an important session because you've invited me three times!"), and it reminds participants who might have forgotten about the session. This phone call can be as simple as saying, "Just wanted to remind you that we are looking forward to seeing you tomorrow at 2 p.m. at the library to talk about neighborhood recycling."

Incentives to Participate

Incentives are needed because it takes effort to participate in a focus group. The participant must reserve a time on his or her schedule and then promise to hold that time open for the group. For individuals whose lives are unpredictable or who are subject to the wishes of others, this can be a big promise. Furthermore, the participants typically incur financial and emotional expenses to participate—child care, travel, having to leave their kids when they feel like they don't spend enough time with them anyway, having to be inside on a beautiful day, having to leave home after they have just settled into their favorite chair, or the apprehension of talking about something dear or personal to them. Finally, the participant spends a designated amount of time in the focus group. This level of individual contribution exceeds that needed for other forms of data gathering. The mail-out survey and the telephone interview are conducted in the participant's home or office, and no travel is necessary. With the mail-out survey and, to a lesser extent, the telephone interview, the participant has some choice about when he or she will respond. Furthermore, surveys and telephone interviews rarely take two hours. Individual interviews come closest to the focus group in terms of the investment the participant must make. However, with individual interviews, the participant is a partner in setting the time and location of the interview, usually within the home or office of the interviewee at a time convenient for him or her.

Focus groups are unique from other data-gathering processes in terms of the investment that must be made by the individual. It is therefore no surprise that a tradition has been established to provide an incentive for participation. From a practical aspect, it would be next to impossible to conduct focus groups without incentives in some situations.

The incentive is not a reward and not really an honorarium or salary. It is an incentive! It serves as a stimulus to attend the session. The primary function of the incentive is to get the participants to show up for the focus group—and to show up on time. The motivational influence of the incentive hasn't worked if the participants are surprised when they receive it. Imagine yourself coming home from a hard day's work. You're tired. You're hungry. Your day didn't go well. You're looking forward to a relaxing evening at home. But you promised someone a couple of weeks ago that you would go to a small group discussion tonight. Now this is one of the times when the incentive kicks in. You recall what was promised if you attend, and you decide that it will be worth the effort to go. Another way the incentive works is to encourage participants to hold open the time of the scheduled focus group. Some people will receive a number of last-minute requests for the same time period. The incentive serves to protect the promised time slot from being preempted. The third function of the incentive is to communicate to the participants that the focus group is important.

By far the most common type of incentive is money. Money has several advantages. Its value is immediately recognized and understood by the participants, it is portable, it will fit into small spaces, and, most important, it works. We give each participant an envelope with cash in it at the conclusion of the group. We have each person sign a form with the date and name of the sponsoring organization that says something such as, "I received $50 for participating in a discussion about nature areas." Immediate payment in cash is preferred. The promise of a check in the mail within a few weeks will be a disappointment. The amount of the payment can and should vary—but not within the same focus group. Each person within a particular group and sometimes within the total study should receive equivalent payment. You don't want to create the impression that some people's opinions are worth more than others' opinions. When considering the amount of payment, the researcher should be mindful of the workable range. At the lower end of the range, the researcher risks insulting the participants with a payment that is too small. Although this will vary, promises of payments in the range of $10 to $15 may be too low and be a detriment to the project. When time and travel are considered, it may be below minimum wage and just not enough to be taken seriously. Better to be creative and come up with another type of incentive. At the upper end of the range, the researcher will find that the study can quickly get too expensive, and the participants may feel awkward receiving what they perceive to be an excessive payment—especially from a public or nonprofit organization.

Generally, as the payment approaches the ceiling, the time needed to recruit is reduced. In some studies, it may be more efficient to pay more for incentives and thereby reduce the recruiting time and the likelihood that people won't show up. At the time of this writing, amounts of $25 to $50 usually work for public and nonprofit studies. As the amount approaches $50, an interesting phenomenon begins to occur. If the participant has a last-minute conflict, he or she is more likely to call the moderator and offer to send a replacement in his or her absence. When working with elite categories of focus group participants, the amounts may need to be adjusted upward. Focus groups with engineers, physicians, attorneys, upper management, and similar categories may require amounts in the $100 to $200+ range.

When asked why they participate in focus groups, 66% of those surveyed indicated compensation as the main motivator based on a study by Rodgers Marketing Research in Canton, Ohio ("Money Not the Only Motivation," 1991, p. 17). Money is not the only incentive

EXAMPLE

An Effective Nonfinancial Incentive

This doesn't come from a focus group study, but it is a good example of providing a gift that doesn't cost much but that people treasure. Several years ago, a researcher was sending out a burdensome survey to private forest landowners. Because the survey was lengthy, the research team was concerned that the respondents would not reply. Considerable discussion was given to an incentive to participate. A number of items were suggested and rejected. Finally one of the team members had a clever idea. "Up at the Forestry School, we have a garbage can full of tree seeds. But not just any seeds. Back a number of years ago we were experimenting with hybrid spruce trees. We interbred a red, white, and blue spruce, and the result was called the 'All American Spruce.' The new tree didn't possess the fea- tures we wanted, and as a result, we couldn't commercially market the tree. We have lots of the seed, and we could put this seed in small envelopes along with a note describing the development. Maybe the forest owners would consider it interesting." The comment was a huge understatement. Inadvertently, we dis- covered that we had given the forest owners an object of major value. It reinforced their values and couldn't be obtained anywhere else at any cost. The respondents wrote back and asked for more seeds. They put the pack- ets on their coffee tables. Some even framed the seeds. The seeds were about to be dumped out because they were considered garbage by the researchers, but to those receiving the seeds, they were a gift beyond value.

that works, and in some cases, it can be inappropriate or illegal. Employees released from work to attend a focus group are already being compensated, and financial incentives are usually deemed inappropriate, if not illegal.

The incentive is symbolic, and other symbols may be worthy substitutes. Food, which can range from light snacks to a full meal, can be effective. Gifts can work well, but they must be adequately described in advance to avoid disappointment when they are presented. Sometimes gifts can be of limited financial value but have significant emotional or psychological value.

A positive and upbeat invitation, the opportunity to share opinions, meals or refreshments, and tangible gifts are all incentives we've used. So is a convenient, comfortable, and easy-to-find meeting location. For some target audiences, it is important to know they will be participating in a research project in which their opinions will be of particular value. They feel honored when they are asked to provide opinions for a research project. Finally, people are more likely to attend a focus group if the invitation builds on some existing community, social, or personal relationship. Thus, an invitation might mention the connection between the study and a local organization, social cause, or respected individual.

SUMMARY

Who should be invited? How do you find them? How do you get them to show up? These are the questions answered by this chapter. You need the right number of the right people to show up for a focus group to be successful. Homogeneity is the guiding principle for focus groups, and the researcher must determine the nature of that homogeneity based on the purpose of the study. Potential participants can be located in a variety of ways, including lists or directories, through cooperating organizations or individuals, or on location at an event or activity.

Be thoughtful about setting the screens for recruitment. These help ensure that you are getting the right people. Think carefully about how you want to describe the study and its benefits to potential participants. Does it sound inviting? Worthwhile? Nonthreatening? Use a systematic recruitment strategy that is repetitive and personalized. Use a combination of incentives to get people to say yes to the invitation and to get them out of their recliners and to the focus group. Incentives can vary and need not be limited to money, although cash does work well. If you don't have cash, be creative.

PRACTICE HINT

Practice Hint 4.1

Telephone Screening Questionnaire:
Department of Health Focus Groups Recruitment Script

(THIS IS MEANT ONLY AS A GUIDE. DON'T READ THIS AS YOU INVITE PEOPLE. YOUR CALL SHOULD SOUND CONVERSATIONAL.)

Name of person _____

Phone number _____

Time called _____

Better time to call _____

Hi, this is (your name) and I'm with (name of agency). We're working with the Minnesota Department of Health to design a new program for new parents. I got your name from (name a person or agency), and they said you might be interested in what we are doing. We want to talk with new moms. You're a new mom, right? (Could chat about how old the baby is, etc.)

We're getting together a small group of moms to give us input on how to design a new home visiting program. We are trying to get ideas about what new moms would like. We plan to get about eight moms together. It will be:

Date, day
Time (two hours)
Place

We will have a few refreshments and we will have $40 for you as a thank you for giving us your time and ideas. We will also have child care available, if you want to bring your children.
Would you be able to join us?

No_____   OK. Thanks for your time.
Yes_____   Great. I'd like to send you a letter just to confirm everything.

I have (check spelling of the name from above and get address)

Address _____

_____

Will you need child care?   No_____

Yes_____ OK.   Just to help us plan for the child care, what are the names and ages of the children you will be bringing along?

_____

_____

Great. I'll send out the letter and we look forward to seeing you at the discussion.

Practice Hint 4.2

Follow-Up Recruitment Letter

[Date]

Sara Olson
101 Maxwell Ave.
Bogus, MN 12345

Thank you for accepting our invitation to talk about designing a home visiting program for new parents. The Department of Health is creating this program for people like you. We want advice about what you would like, what will work, and what won't work. It doesn't matter if you have had home visits or not. We're interested in the ideas of all moms with new babies. The group will be held:

> Tuesday, May 14
> 2 to 4 p.m.
> Burns County Department of Health Building
> 1494 Idaho Avenue West in Spooner, just around the corner from Nick's Café
> Room 102—just inside the front door and to the right

It will be a small group, about eight people. We've got great child care arranged for Megan and Max. Several teachers from the Early Childhood Family Education program have agreed to watch the little ones. We'll bring snacks for you and the kids, and we'll have $40 for you at the end of the session.

If for some reason you won't be able to join us, please call as soon as possible so we can invite someone else. If you have any questions, give me a call at 624-2221.

We are looking forward to meeting you, Megan, and Max next Tuesday. See you then.

Sincerely,

Kathy Graf
Health Consultant

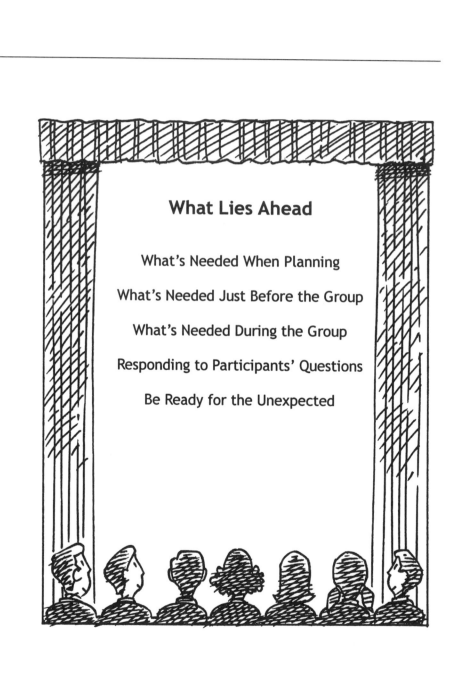

5

Moderating Skills

$\mathbf{M}$uch of the success of the focused interview depends on well-developed questions asked of the right respondents, but another ingredient is essential—a skillful moderator. Interviewing looks deceptively simple but requires preparation, mental discipline, and group interaction skills.

What's Needed When Planning

Selecting the Right Moderator

Who should moderate the focus groups? Sometimes it is an automatic decision. It is the principal investigator, the head researcher, the person who did focus groups last time, or a staff member who wants to gain experience with focus groups. Don't limit yourself to these choices. Consider the skills needed for the task as well as the preferences and characteristics of your target audience. Listed below are some factors that we've found to be important.

Moderators' respect for participants may be one of the most influential factors affecting the quality of focus group results. The moderator must believe that the participants have wisdom no matter what their level of education, experience, or background. Indeed, they may have limited knowledge on the topic, hold opposing values to that of the researchers, or seem to have fuzzy logic, but the moderator listens attentively with sensitivity, trying to understand their perspective. Often after the fourth or fifth group, the moderator will have heard the topic discussed in a variety of ways, and many of the concerns and key ideas will have been said several times. At this point, some information is old stuff to the moderator, but it still deserves the respect and active listening that were present the first time it was heard. Lack of respect quickly telegraphs to the participants and essentially shuts down meaningful communication. Why share your personal feelings when the moderator seems dismissive?

We've observed hundreds of moderators over the years and found that respect can be communicated in a variety of ways. In fact, we've worked with colleagues who do, indeed, care deeply about the participants but had difficulty exhibiting signals. The signals are the little things that let participants know that you care about them. The moderator shows interest in their lives and what is happening in their environment. The moderator interacts informally before and possibly after the focus group. The moderator looks at participants and gives the appearance of active listening. Some moderators will lean forward as they listen; others will take notes of key points. The moderator is not dismissive of comments and makes an effort to listen to each person in the group. The moderator shouldn't see moderating as a "job" that needs to get done but as an honor that he or she gets to hear what these people have to say on the topic.

Empathy and positive regard are critical qualities of the moderator. This attitude must permeate the entire focus group environment. Here's a meditation developed by Jack Kornfield that reflects how we

TIP

Show That You Care

It is not enough that the moderator cares about the participants. This concern must be reflected in behaviors that are observable to those in the focus group. We once did a study for a large medical facility that wanted to know what patients looked for in their health care. Over and over we heard patients say they knew they received good care when they felt the doctors and nurses cared about them as people. We asked patients to tell us how they could tell when the staff cared. Patients described how caregivers would stop them in the hallway and ask how they were doing. They took time to listen. Also, it was particularly meaningful when the caregivers remembered the patient's name and asked about family members or events in the patient's life. These concrete ways were signs to patients that their medical providers cared about them. And they felt that when the caregivers cared about them as people, then they got good health care. Moderators also need to go beyond saying they care and show it by their behavior.

try to approach moderating focus groups. We hope that those planning to moderate might find it beneficial.

> Picture or imagine that this earth is filled with Buddhas, that every single being you encounter is enlightened, except one— yourself! Imagine that they are all here to teach you. Whoever you encounter is acting as they do solely for your benefit, to provide just the teachings and difficulties you need in order to awaken.
>
> Sense what lessons they offer to you. Inwardly thank them for this. Throughout a day or a week continue to develop the image of enlightened teachers all around you. Notice how it changes your whole perspective on life. (Kornfield, 1993, p. 82)

The moderator must have adequate background knowledge on the topic of discussion to place comments in perspective and follow up on critical areas of concern. Some successful moderators are able to use naïveté to an advantage by prompting participants to amplify their comments, but if used in excess, it can become tiresome and inhibit complicated responses. Naïveté is a two-edged sword. In some circumstances, it elicits considerable new information that may have been assumed—sometimes incorrectly—by the moderator. Furthermore, it can produce eloquent statements that place the topic of discussion into a larger context. Unfortunately, this same tactic can become infuriating to knowledgeable participants who feel the moderator has not yet earned the right to ask questions.

The moderator must be able to communicate clearly in writing and orally. The questions asked by the moderator are the backbone of the focused interview, and if these questions are convoluted or confusing, or reflect fuzzy thinking, then the entire process is in jeopardy.

Moderating requires the ability to listen and the self-discipline to control your personal views. Focus groups have been jeopardized because novice moderators could not hold back their own opinions. Moderators who have a personal commitment to the topic need to be careful to keep their personal views to themselves and focus on understanding the perceptions of the group participants. It's hard to listen to people who don't know the program as well as you do or who criticize a program near and dear to your heart. Harder yet is to smile and say "thank you" after they've ripped up your sacred program. Some moderators make the mistake of defending or explaining rather than just listening. Professional focus group moderators have a distinct advantage in this respect because they are emotionally detached from the topic of the study. It is easier to be open and listen.

Participants must feel comfortable with the moderator. They should feel that the moderator is the appropriate person to ask the questions and that the answers can be openly discussed. There are few absolutes about the physical characteristics of the moderator because much depends on the situation and the past experiences of the participants. It is more than having the participants comfortable with the moderator's dress and appearance. Consideration should be given to factors such as gender, race, age, language, socioeconomic characteristics, technical knowledge, and perceived power differences. Each of these, depending on the circumstances, has the potential for inhibiting communication. A simple example is that it is probably easier for men to talk about prostate problems with a male moderator than with a female moderator.

The moderator is a person, a member of a racial group, an age category, a gender, and so on, and any one of these factors could inhibit or prompt openness within the group. A valuable asset of many nonprofit and public institutions is the ability to recruit volunteer moderators who are not researchers but who possess the characteristics essential for success.

Finally, a friendly manner and a sense of humor are valuable assets. Just a smile from the moderator can help people feel like this might be an OK experience. Smiles typically connote warmth, caring, and empathy and are powerful factors in promoting conversation. Humor is a powerful bonding agent, particularly when it is spontaneous and not at anyone's expense. Excessive efforts at humor can fall flat, be

CAUTION

Keep Questions Clear

Sometimes in an effort to be helpful, the moderator will ask a question in several different ways. The moderator usually assumes that this strategy helps the participant, but in fact, it often does just the opposite. If the questions are perceived as different, then respondents become confused with the intent. Moreover, it makes analysis difficult because you are not sure which question was actually answered.

misinterpreted, and be counterproductive. However, if someone says something funny, don't hold back your laugh.

The Moderating Team

Consider using a moderator team: a moderator and an assistant moderator. Each has certain tasks to perform. The moderator is primarily concerned with directing the discussion, keeping the conversation flowing, and taking a few notes. The notes of the moderator are not so much to capture the total interview but rather to identify a few key ideas, to remember comments to be rewoven into the later conversation, or to jot down questions that might be asked at the end of the group. The assistant, on the other hand, takes comprehensive notes, operates the tape recorder, handles the environmental conditions and logistics (refreshments, lighting, seating, etc.), and responds to unexpected interruptions. Near the end of the discussion, the moderator may ask the assistant if he or she wants to ask any additional questions or follow up on anything. The assistant may be asked to give a short (two-minute) summary of the key points of the discussion. Also, the assistant is key during the postmeeting analysis of the session.

The assistant moderator is not usually used in private sector market research projects unless as an apprentice. This limited use of assistant moderators is due to additional labor and travel costs. We have found assistant moderators well worth the investment in the public and nonprofit environment, particularly in situations when you do not have the special rooms with one-way mirrors. A second set of eyes and ears increases both the total accumulation of information and the validity of the analysis. Furthermore, an assistant provides a means for dealing with distracting interruptions to the focus group interview, such as latecomers, unwanted background music, or switching tapes.

Public and nonprofit organizations have a potential advantage in the use of assistant moderators. Within many organizations, individuals are willing to "sit in" on the focus group due to curiosity or concern and help with assigned functions. In some circumstances, these individuals may have background characteristics similar to those of the participants, and as a result, they may offer valuable assistance in analysis. Some care must be taken to ensure that the newly recruited assistant moderator understands the roles and responsibilities and doesn't inadvertently upstage the focus group. This can be solved by explicitly outlining the purpose and rules of the session. An example of assistant moderator responsibilities is included in Practice Hint 5.2.

EXAMPLE

Getting the Right Moderator

An AIDS researcher was planning on conducting focus group interviews with prostitutes who were also intravenous drug users. The topic was on the use of condoms and sterilized needles in AIDS prevention. This situation presented difficulties to the focus group researchers, who understood little of the culture or environment of the target audience. Also, the researchers would have to spend a great deal of time developing trust with the prostitutes. The best strategy in this situation may be to enlist the help of a drug-using prostitute to moderate the focus groups.

What's Needed Just Before the Group

Mental Preparation

Moderators must be mentally alert and free from distractions, anxieties, or pressures that would limit their ability to think quickly. Moderating a group discussion requires concentration and careful listening. Therefore, plan your schedule to minimize pressures that would limit your ability to concentrate (e.g., get enough sleep, don't fight with your teenagers, don't do more than two groups in one day). Moderators must be able to give their full attention to the group.

The moderator should be completely familiar with the introduction and the questioning route. Practice saying the introduction and questions aloud while in the shower or while driving. Get comfortable with the questions. Know why you are asking each question. Know how much time you expect to spend on each question. Know which questions are key questions. You want to sound conversational. You don't want to sound like you have it memorized, and you don't want to read it word for word. Glancing at the questioning route to remember the next question is tolerable, but reading the question (and taking eyes off the participants) destroys the spontaneous flow of the discussion.

Another aspect of mental preparation is the discipline of listening and thinking simultaneously. It is just not enough to be an empty vessel, listening and absorbing the comments of participants. If you do, you will end up with a fair amount of trivia. The skillful moderator listens and then knows just when to push the participants a bit farther or ask a probing question. This skillful moderator doesn't automatically believe everything that is said but, instead, compares it to what was expected or to what was said by others in previous focus groups. One of the critical moderator skills is knowing when and how to seek amplification. Sometimes participants intellectualize an answer—talking about how something could or should be done or giving a theoretical response instead of one based on their actual experience. Other times, participants will speak in cliches. Or sometimes the participant's response seems to be completely disconnected from the question. These digressions and mental detours are relatively easy to spot when you leisurely listen to the audiotape the next day but difficult to catch at the moment they are said. With practice, this becomes easier.

Without a doubt, the moderating process is hard work and fatiguing. Because of the mental and emotional discipline required, we don't conduct more than two focus groups on the same day. By the third

TIP

Be Alert: Are They Answering the Question?

Beginning moderators are so darn glad that people are talking that they sometimes miss that people aren't answering the question they asked. Participants may be answering an earlier question. Or they may be off on a tangent. Or they may be skirting the question. It may all be fascinating, but it may not be answering the question. The moderator has to be mentally alert to spot this and must bring the group back to the question.

group, it is hard to remember if something was said in this group or an earlier group. Also, allow sufficient time between focus groups to reenergize.

Pre-Session Strategy

Everything should be set up and ready for the group when the first participant arrives. If you are still fiddling with the recorder or writing on the flip chart, it makes some people uncomfortable. The moderating team then act as hosts. We think of it as what we do when we welcome people to our home. We greet them at the door. Welcome them. Introduce ourselves. We introduce them to one another. We do whatever we can to help them feel comfortable. We offer refreshments and make small talk. Sometimes we split our roles. One will act as the greeter; the other will take care of any paperwork. Occasionally participants are asked to fill out a short registration form that asks questions about demographic characteristics, particularly those characteristics that we don't want to discuss within the group. In some situations, we have a human subjects form for them to sign as they arrive. Even if we have them filling out paperwork, the emphasis is on creating a friendly, warm, and comfortable environment.

Small talk helps put the participants at ease, but avoid the key issues to be discussed later in the session. If participants explain their perceptions in the informal part of the meeting, they may be reluctant to repeat their observations during the group. Purposeful small talk avoids the focused issue and instead concentrates on common human experiences such as weather, children, or sports. Avoid controversial topics (religion, politics, or sensitive local issues) and topics that highlight differences within the group (income, education, political influence, etc.).

Because participants arrive at different times, the small talk maintains the warm and friendly environment until a sufficient number of participants are present to begin the session. In most situations, this small-talk period will last only five to ten minutes, and the two-person moderating team should plan their welcoming strategy in advance. Often, if no paperwork needs to be taken care of, the moderator or assistant moderator meets the participants at the door and brings them into the social gathering while the other person on the team visits with the group.

During this period, the moderator and assistant are observing participant interaction and noting individuals who tend to dominate the group, those who consider themselves as experts, or people who

TIP

Practice Small Talk

Qualities that make someone good at academic research may be different from qualities that make for good field research. Some researchers are uncomfortable and feel awkward when they meet people, and it shows. Let members of the research team practice the small talk with each other. Let those who have this gift coach others who seek to develop it.

seem shy or quiet. Individuals who talk a lot may later dominate the conversation and should be seated at the moderator's side if possible. Then, if necessary, the moderator can turn slightly away from the domineering individuals, thereby giving a nonverbal and diplomatic signal for others to talk. Shy and quiet participants are best placed immediately across from the moderator to facilitate maximum eye contact. The moderator might expect that about 40% of the participants would be eager and open to sharing insights, and another 40% are more introspective and willing to talk if the situation presents itself. The remaining 20% are apprehensive about the experience and rarely share (Kelleher, 1982).

This strategic positioning of participants is achieved in the following manner. The moderating team will have a list of participants who are expected to attend the discussion and will prepare "name tents" to place on the table in front of group members. Name tents can easily be made from 5-by-8-inch index cards, folded in the middle with first names printed. Last names aren't necessary. Name tents are preferred because they are larger and more legible than nametags. The moderator will casually "drop" the name tents around the table in a seemingly random manner. In fact, the moderator arranges the cards using observations from the informal pre-session, quickly checks perceptions with the assistant moderator, and then places the name tents.

Snacks and Meals

Food can help the focus group. Eating together tends to promote conversation and communication within the group. Most focus groups use a variety of snacks, such as cookies or pastries or fruit and vegetable

trays, but full meals also can be effective. Snacks and light refreshments are typically placed on a table to the side of the room and are enjoyed during the pre-session small talk and during the discussion. Full meals require additional planning. If they are conducted in restaurants, then advance arrangements are needed to ensure speedy service. Meals can be catered or delivered (e.g., pizza, box lunches). Thought should be given to when the meal is served. Traditional protocol was that the meal should occur before the focus group as a way for the participants to get to know each other. This can be awkward as the moderator tries to avoid the central topic of discussion. An alternative strategy is to provide the meal after the focus group, during which time the moderator continues to listen for relevant comments concerning the study.

What's Needed During the Group
Recording the Group Discussion

Focus groups are typically recorded in two ways: by a tape recorder and with written notes. Written notes are essential. Typically the moderator will take a few notes, but note taking is really the role of the assistant who tries to capture complete statements of the participants—especially those comments that may be quotable. The note taking should not interfere with the spontaneous nature of the group interview, and only the moderator will be able to capture brief comments by participants. If the group has to wait until the moderator finishes taking notes, the discussion will hardly be free-flowing. Also, some participants wonder why the moderator takes notes on some statements and not on others.

Notes should be as complete as possible in case the tape recorder doesn't work. Tape recorders shouldn't be completely trusted. Murphy's Law dictates that the most insightful comment will be lost when the tape is being switched or when background noise drowns out voices on the tape. At times, the moderator and assistant moderator may get so involved in the discussion that they both forget to monitor the tape recorder.

Set up the tape-recording equipment and remote microphone before the meeting begins and in plain sight of participants. Hidden recorders and microphones are usually unwise because they create an unnecessarily secretive atmosphere. Introduce the recorder at the beginning of the discussion as a tool to help capture everyone's comments.

Avoid excessive attention to the tape recording. Occasionally, a novice moderator will appear nervous at this point—avoiding eye contact, stumbling over the explanation of taping, and commenting at length about the tape recording. Inadvertently, the moderator creates an environment that restricts the free flow of information due to

TIP

Serve Quiet Food

Veteran moderators have found that some meals are noisy and make it difficult to get clear sound on the tape recorder. Avoid glass, china, cans, and silverware. Instead, use paper cups and plates with plastic forks and spoons.

overattention to recording. It is usually best to mention the recording and confidentiality and move on to the next topic. However, in work situations, participants may need more information, such as who will get to listen to the tape and how it will be used. In some situations, the tape recording is perceived as symbolic of careful listening.

EXAMPLE

The Tape Recorder Is a Signal of Listening

A large school system conducted focus groups on merit pay of teachers—a sensitive topic to most teachers. In the planning phase, some people on the study team were concerned that tape recording would inhibit conversation. The decision was made to try it and, if necessary, turn off the recording equipment. When the teachers arrived for the first focus group, one of the first comments was, "Finally the school administration is taking the opinions of teachers seriously." The moderator asked the teacher to comment further. The reply: "Well, you're tape recording our comments! All along the school administrators said they were listening and we knew they weren't because they didn't record, take notes, or anything. Now it looks like they are serious about listening." When topics of concern were addressed in the groups, the teachers would lean toward the microphone in the center of the table and talk slowly so that their comments would be clearly understood.

Getting great sound quality is difficult because recorders tend to pick up tapping of pencils and the hum of the ventilation system instead of the softly spoken comments of participants. Built-in microphones on cassette recorders don't pick up group discussions well, and their recordings are hard to listen to. Instead, we use an omnidirectional, pressure sensitive remote microphone placed in the center of the table. Pressure sensitive microphones pick up sound vibrations from the table. Occasionally, moderators use two microphones placed at different ends of the table, each connected to a recorder. Before people arrive for the group interview, the moderator should test recording equipment to be sure that all comments in the room will be captured, even if spoken in quiet tones.

Other ways are also being used to capture focus group results. Video cameras are more compact than ever before, but still they are obtrusive. We rarely use them. Another method is to digitally record the focus group onto a laptop computer using special software and then mark selected choice parts for later review and analysis (Belisle, 1998, p. 18). Still another strategy is to have a fast typist transcribe the focus group in real time. Voice recognition software is steadily improving and can transcribe voices that have been "trained" to be recognized by the software. In the near future, this software may be able to distinguish between multiple voices and offer immediate transcripts.

Beginning the Focus Group Discussion

The first few moments in a focus group discussion are critical. In this brief time, the moderator must give enough information so people feel comfortable with the topic, create a permissive atmosphere, provide the ground rules, and set the tone of the discussion. Much of the success of group interviewing can be attributed to this three- to five-minute introduction. Being too formal or rigid can stifle interaction among participants. By contrast, too much informality and humor can cause problems because participants might not take the discussion seriously. Veteran moderators testify that groups are unpredictable, and one group may be exciting and free-flowing, whereas another group might be low energy or cautious. Differences between groups should be expected; however, the moderator should introduce the group discussion in a consistent manner.

The recommended pattern for introducing the group discussion includes the following:

1. The welcome
2. The overview of the topic
3. The ground rules (or things that will help our discussion go smoothly)
4. The first question

Here is an example of a typical introduction:

Good evening and welcome. Thanks for taking the time to join our discussion of airplane travel. My name is Pete Krueger, and I represent the Happy Traveler Research Agency. Assisting me is Sheree Benson, also from the Happy Traveler Agency. We have been asked by the airline industry to help them get some information about how public employees feel about airline travel. They want the information to help them improve the service they provide.

You were invited because you are all government employees who work here in the metropolitan area and you have all flown at least four times in the past year. We want to tap into those experiences and your opinions about airline travel.

There are no right or wrong answers. We expect that you will have differing points of view. Please feel free to share your point of view even if it differs from what others have said.

We're tape recording the session because we don't want to miss any of your comments. No names will be included in any reports. Your comments are confidential. Keep in mind that we're just as interested in negative comments as positive comments, and at times the negative comments are the most helpful.

We have name tents here in front of us tonight. They help me remember names, but they can also help you. If you want to follow up on something that someone has said, you want to agree, or disagree, or give an example, feel free to do that. Don't feel like you have to respond to me all the time. Feel free to have a conversation with one another about these questions. I am here to ask questions, listen, and make sure everyone has a chance to share. We're interested in hearing from each of you. So if you're talking a lot, I may ask you to give others a chance. And if you aren't saying much, I may call on you. We just want to make sure we hear from all of you.

Feel free to get up and get more refreshments if you would like. Let's begin. Let's find out some more about each other by going around the room one at a time. Tell us your name and some of the places that you've flown to in the past year.

The first question is designed to get all participants to say something early in the conversation. It breaks the ice. After the participant has said something, it is more likely that he or she will speak again. In addition, the first question underscores the common characteristics of the participants and that they all have some basis for sharing information. This first question must be the type that can be answered in about thirty seconds and, as a result, will often consist of factual information. Furthermore, this first question cannot demand excessive reflection or long-past memories.

Anticipating the Flow of the Discussion

Group discussions are unpredictable. The discussion might flow precisely as planned, or it might take leaps and detours. Try to anticipate

CAUTION

Don't Invite Questions at the Beginning of the Focus Group

It is risky to ask the participants if they have questions when you begin the focus group. Unfortunately, these early participant questions may preempt the discussion and place the moderator in a defensive position. When confronted by certain questions, the moderator will appear apologetic and uncertain of the study. Examples include the following: "Who really wants this information? Are you really going to use what we tell you? Who else are you talking to? Why aren't you talking to X? What did X say? Can we see copies of the report?" Instead, don't invite questions at the beginning. If someone does ask a question, the moderator might indicate that the topic will come later in the discussion. For more ideas, see the section later in this chapter on "Participant Questions."

the various directions the discussion might take and recognize beneficial topics of discussion as opposed to dead ends. For example, in focus groups relating to community organizations, we have found that the discussion often leads to an evaluation of agency professionals—a topic that isn't the purpose of the study. In these cases, it is helpful to include a comment in the introduction about the scope of the study. "We are more interested in your opinions about programs, building facilities, and activities and less concerned about the people who deliver those services." Often a "mock discussion" with colleagues familiar with the participants will help identify some of the varieties of responses.

Sometimes participants will jump ahead and start talking about a question that comes later in your questioning route. They may start talking about Question 7 when you are still on Question 4. You need to decide whether to let the conversation move to Question 7 (which may be perfectly fine, but you'll want to return to Questions 5 and 6) or whether you want to bring them back to Question 4 right away. Expect these leaps. Know where you are going well enough to know if altering the flow matters.

Two Essential Techniques: The Pause and the Probe

Moderators of group discussions should be familiar with two essential techniques: the five-second pause and the probe. Both techniques are easy to use and helpful in drawing additional information from group participants. The five-second pause is often used after a participant comment. This short pause often prompts additional points of view or agreement with the previously mentioned position. There is a tendency for novice moderators to talk too much or to move too quickly from one topic to another, usually because they feel uncomfortable with silence. Often the short pause will elicit additional points of view, especially when coupled with eye contact from the moderator. Practice the five-second pause on family, friends, and coworkers. It allows you to become comfortable with this technique.

The second essential technique is the probe—the request for additional information. In most conversations and group discussions, there is a tendency for people to make vague comments that could have multiple meanings or to say "I agree." When this occurs, the probe is an effective technique to elicit additional information. Typically, probing involves comments such as the following:

- Would you explain further?
- Would you give me an example of what you mean?
- Would you say more?
- Tell us more.
- Say more.
- Is there anything else?
- Please describe what you mean.
- I don't understand.

Use the probe a few times early in the interview to communicate the importance of precision in responses. For example, if a participant indicates agreement by saying, "I agree," then the moderator should follow up with, "Tell us more," or "What experiences have you had that make you feel that way?" A few probes used in this way underscore the impression that more detailed answers are wanted. Excessive probing, however, can be time-consuming, annoying, and unnecessary.

Participants may need to be reminded of the value of differing points of view. The introduction provides the first suggestion that all points of view are needed and wanted. A second reminder is helpful if the moderator senses that participants are simply "echoing" the same concept. After several echoes on the same idea, the moderator might ask, "Does anyone see it differently?" or "Has anyone had a different experience?" or "Are there other points of view?"

TIP

Think Past, Present, and Future

Successful moderators think about what has already been discussed, what is currently being said, and what still needs to be covered. This helps them take in the whole scope of the focus group and keep the discussion on track and on schedule.

Experts, Dominant Talkers, Shy Participants, and Ramblers

One of the exciting aspects of focus group discussions is that they bring together people with different backgrounds and characteristics. However, individual characteristics can present challenges for the moderator. Four types of participants—the expert, the dominant talker, the shy participant, and the rambler—present challenges.

Self-appointed "experts" can present special problems in focus groups. What they say and how they say it can inhibit others in the group. Participants often defer to others who are perceived to have more experience or are better informed on a topic. Some people consider themselves experts because they have had considerable experience with the topic, because they hold positions of influence in the community, or because they have previously participated in this type of session. Often the best way of handling experts is to underscore the fact that everyone is an expert and all participants have important perceptions that need to be expressed. In addition, the introductory question should avoid responses that would highlight participants' levels of education, affluence, years of experience with the topic, or social or political influence.

Dominant talkers sometimes consider themselves to be experts, but much of the time, they are unaware of how they are perceived by others. Often dominant talkers are spotted in pre-session small talk. As indicated earlier in this chapter, try to seat the dominant individual beside the moderator to exercise control by the use of body language. When this strategy does not work, then the more frontal tactic of verbally shifting attention is required. For example, "Thank you, John. Are there others who wish to comment on the question?" or "Does anyone feel differently?" or "That's one point of view. Does anyone have another point of view?" Other nonverbal techniques also can be used, such as avoiding eye contact with the talker. Most important, be tactful and kind, because harsh comments may curtail spontaneity from others in the group.

Shy respondents and reflective thinkers tend to say little. It seems that these participants think carefully first and then speak. By contrast, others in the group are thinking and speaking at the same time. Shy and reflective participants often have great insights, but it takes extra effort to get them to elaborate their views. If possible, the moderator should place shy respondents directly across the table to maximize eye contact. Eye contact often provides sufficient encouragement to speak, and if all else fails, the moderator can call on them by name. "Tom, I don't want to leave you out of the conversation. What do you think?"

Rambling respondents use a lot of words and take forever to get to the point, if they have a point. These individuals like to talk. Unfortunately, the rambling respondent is off track a fair amount of the time and can eat up precious discussion time. As a rule of thumb, we usually discontinue eye contact with the rambler after about twenty to thirty seconds. The assistant moderator should do likewise. Look at your papers, look at the other participants, turn your body away from the speaker, but don't look at the rambler. As soon as the rambler stops or pauses, the moderator should be ready to fire away with the next question or repeat the current question being discussed. In the remainder of the discussion, the moderating team may want to limit eye contact with the rambling individual.

Some moderators include a statement in the introduction that alerts participants to the importance of hearing from everyone. "From past experience in groups like this, we know that some people talk a lot, and some people don't say much. It is important that we hear from all of you because you've had different experiences. So if you are talking a lot, I may interrupt you, and if you aren't saying much, I may call on you. If I do, please don't feel bad about it. It is just my way of making sure we get through all the questions and that everyone has a chance to talk."

Don't assume that everyone should talk the same amount in a focus group. Some participants will just have more to say than others. If a participant is on track and giving helpful information, we usually let him or her continue to talk. However, we will take action if he or she is rambling or limiting the opportunity for others to talk.

Responding to Participants' Comments

Moderators should be attentive to how they respond to comments from participants—both verbal and nonverbal. Often moderator responses are unconscious habits. Self-discipline and practice are needed to overcome habits such as head nodding and short verbal responses.

Head Nodding

Some moderators will continually nod their head as comments are being made. If it is a slow continuous nod given to everyone, it often signals encouragement: "I'm listening, keep going." However, if it is a fast head nod, it probably signals agreement and, as a result, tends to elicit additional comments of the same type. As a rule of thumb, beginning moderators should try to restrict head nodding.

Short Verbal Responses

In many of our social interactions, we have become conditioned to provide short verbal responses that signal approval or acceptance. Many of these are acceptable within the focus group environment such as "OK," "Yes," or "Uh huh," but others should be avoided if they communicate indications of accuracy or agreement. Responses to avoid include "Correct," "That's good," or "Excellent" because they imply judgments about the quality of the comment.

Concluding the Focus Group

The moderator has several options for closing the focus group. Perhaps the most common procedure is simply to thank the group for participating, provide them with the gift or cash if promised, and wish them a safe journey home. A far better alternative is for the assistant moderator or the moderator to briefly summarize the main points and ask if this summary is accurate. This is helpful in the subsequent analysis process. It is the first opportunity the research team has to pull together a summary of the group discussion. When presenting the brief summary, the researchers should watch the body language of the participants for signs of agreement, hesitation, or confusion. When the two- to three-minute summary is completed, the moderator invites comments, amendments, or corrections.

An additional tactic for closure is asking the "final question" that was described in Chapter 3. The moderator provides an overview of the study and then asks the participants, "Have we missed anything?" A variation of this strategy is useful if participants are reluctant to talk because of sensitivity to the recording equipment. An alternative is to turn off the recording equipment, indicate that the discussion is now completed, thank them for their assistance, and then ask, "Do you think we've missed anything in the discussion?" This closure may uncover some avenues of thought that were not anticipated.

TIP

Anticipate Running Out of Time

Before you do the focus group, pretend that you've only asked half of the questions and only ten minutes remain. (We hope this never really happens to you.) Think about options that you might try and how to avoid the situation in the future.

Responding to Participants' Questions

In focus groups, participants sometimes ask questions of the moderator. This should be expected; it is natural, and it can actually be beneficial to the discussion. Questions occur before the focus group, just after the introduction to the focus group, during the focus group, or at the conclusion of the discussion. The strategy of answering differs for each time period.

Questions Before the Focus Group Begins

These questions can occur during the invitation process or just prior to the discussion. These questions are asked individually, and the strategy of answering should be to provide sufficient information to put the participant at ease. Often the questions are about the purpose of the focus group, who's using the results, or about the timing or location. The principle of answering is to give answers but not to give information that might be leading.

Questions After the Introduction

Don't invite these questions. The moderator's introduction usually takes only a few minutes, and you should move directly into the round-robin opening question. Inviting questions at this point is dangerous because there are a number of questions that you may not want to answer until the end of the group. This can make the moderator appear defensive, evasive, and apologetic. The rule of thumb is not to invite questions, but if someone does ask a question, decide if it should be answered or postponed until later.

Questions During the Focus Group

These questions can relate to a variety of topics or concerns. The moderator will need to consider each of these individually. Some should be answered, some should be deflected back to the participant or the group, and some should be postponed.

Questions at the Conclusion of the Group

These questions are welcomed and encouraged. If a question was postponed, be sure to bring it up at the end of the focus group. Here you can tell more about the study—who else you are talking to, what

TIP

How to Answer Participant Questions

When participants ask questions in the focus group, two things go through our minds. Is this really a question? And do I need to give an answer?

Some people use questions to make statements. It sounds like a question, but it isn't. They don't really want an answer. If you sense that the person really wants to make a point, you might respond by saying, " Tell me more about that" or " That's a good question, how would you answer it?" or simply "Why do you ask?"

If the question is indeed a question, then you have several strategies. One strategy is to invite someone else to answer the question. "Would someone like to answer that question?" This is often a desirable strategy if the question is about opinions, rather than facts.

It is important that the moderator doesn't appear evasive. If the question is specifically directed to the moderator, then it is more difficult to give it away.

Another strategy is to postpone the answer. If the topic is going to be discussed in more detail later in the focus group, you might use, "We're going to be talking about that in a few minutes." If the topic is not on the questioning route, you might use, "We'll be talking about things like that at the end. Remind me to talk about that then. But right now our topic is . . ."

Or another strategy is to just answer the question. This is especially true if the question is about a factual matter or something that is an important foundation to later discussion.

---

other groups have said, and how they can get copies of the report. Questions asked at the end of the focus group can give clues about additional information that you might include in the introduction of future focus groups.

Be Ready for the Unexpected

Prepare for the unexpected by thinking about the possible things that can go wrong. Here are some of the things that might go wrong and possible courses of action.

TIP

Can I See a Copy of the Final Report?

Perhaps the most frequently asked question at focus groups, particularly for public and non-profit organizations, is, "Can we get a copy of the results?" Be ready for this question and have a direct answer. Rarely, if ever, are reports shared in the private-market research environment because of the proprietary nature of the results. However, in the public and nonprofit environment, it is wise to allow open access to final reports. Sharing results conveys that you really did listen. Sharing results conveys a sense of openness and fosters positive attitudes that all sides must work together to achieve results. So, anticipate this question and discuss it with the sponsoring group. We recommend that you eagerly share copies of the results. To do this, be sure to maintain a list of names and addresses of all focus group participants. We do not share transcripts, tapes, field notes, or reports of individual focus groups because of our promise of confidentiality. What is shared is a full report or executive summary of the entire study. We are encouraging organizations we work with to include a cover letter that says the following: "We listened. Here are the three, four, or five most important things we heard. This is what we are going to do about it (or this is why we can't do anything about it). Thanks for your input. Call us if you want to tell us anything else."

Hazardous Weather Occurs Just Hours Before the Meeting

Phone each person to let him or her know the session has been canceled.

Nobody Shows Up

Review your letter of invitation to be certain you are at the right location, right date, and right time. Telephone several participants to see if they received the invitation. Always take a list of invited participants with their phone numbers to the discussion location. Try to figure out what went wrong so you can correct it before future groups.

Only a Few Attend

Conduct the session anyway, but after the meeting, check to be certain that all people received the written letter of invitation and telephone reminder. Try to find out what kept people from attending.

The Meeting Place Is Inadequate

Consider adapting or moving, but try to spot this early. Arrive at the interview location well in advance of the participants, especially if it is a location that you have not used before. This gives you time to improvise.

Participants Bring Children

Consider improvising by having a team member serve as baby-sitter, keeping the child in the room, or not including the parent in the focus group. Try to anticipate this before it occurs. Children can make conducting a focus group tough. Young children running in the room or babies crying can completely upstage the discussion, at least from the moderator's perspective. Ideally, this problem is anticipated and planned for. When young parents are the target audience, the moderator should expect that parents will need child care and arrange for child care services. If it wasn't planned for, there are other options. The moderator might make a quick assessment of the child's activity level and decide on the potential for interruptions. If the child is reasonably quiet and not too active, the moderator might decide to include the parent and the child in the discussion. (For example, babies who can't crawl yet are usually fine in a group.) Or the assistant moderator might function as a baby-sitter and take the child into another room. Puzzles, crayons, and coloring books can provide some diversions for children, but it is unreasonable to expect them to be quiet for the entire discussion.

Participants Bring Other Adults

Sometimes participants bring a spouse, a family member, a friend who provided transportation, or someone who they thought would be interested in the topic. The first rule of thumb is to not let the visitor decide whether he or she stays. Chat with anyone who doesn't belong in the group during the pre-session. Then make a decision. Consider finding a place for them to wait or indicating a time when they can return or possibly allowing them to remain in the room. If they fit the screen, we sometimes allow them in the group. Other visitors, such as spouses, might be allowed to sit in the room, often along the side if we don't think it will inhibit the group. Or we may bring along magazines and newspapers and ask the visitors to wait in the lounge or another place while the focus group is taking place.

Other Uninvited People Show Up

Occasionally, someone in a position of authority who is interested in the study shows up. What should you do? Consider thanking them for their interest and offer to get in touch with them later. Some people, such as reporters, are told that this is a research interview and not an open meeting. We tell them we would be willing to talk to them after the group or that we can send them a written report when the study is completed. Others, such as the head of the organization, are thanked for their interest and told that their presence may inhibit the conversation. We ask them to leave.

The Group Doesn't Want to Talk

Consider calling on individuals or going around the group answering a specific question. Use pauses and probes. Take a ten-minute break and reconvene. Ask participants for advice.

The Group Gets So Involved That The Members Don't Want to Leave

Consider staying a while and listening to the conversation. If you absolutely must leave, then formally adjourn the meeting, pack up, and depart. If possible, let the participants remain. This is a delightful problem that does occasionally occur.

The Early Questions Take Too Much Time, Leaving Little Time to Ask the Final Questions

Consider pacing the questions and monitoring the clock during the interview to allow enough time for your final questions. Often the last questions are the most important. You may have to skip some of the middle questions to have time for the key questions.

TIP

Anticipate Running Out of Time

Before you do the focus group, pretend that you've asked only half of the questions and only ten minutes remain. (We hope this never really happens to you.) Think about options that you might try and how to avoid the situation in the future.

SUMMARY

There is a lot to think about in preparing to moderate a focus group interview. The logistics and equipment should be checked out in advance and then crossed off your worry list. Novice moderators sometimes worry about too many things just before the group session and are overly anxious when they begin the group. The best advice for beginning moderators is to practice asking questions, worry several days before the focus group, and then relax just before the discussion.

It's hard to predict how a focus group will go. Groups vary greatly. Throughout the discussion, the moderating team members should remember that they are visitors in the world of the participants, and for a brief time, they are sharing the reality of the participants' environment. The permissive moderator allows the discussion to flow, and topics may be introduced in a different sequence from what was originally anticipated. Anticipate things that can go wrong. Practice pauses and probes and interrupting participants to move the conversation along. Consider the various strategies for bringing closure to the discussion.

Practice Hint 5.1
Checklist for Focus Group Interviews

Advance Notice
_____ Contact participants by phone two weeks (or more) before the session.
_____ Send each participant a letter confirming time, date, and place.
_____ Give the participants a reminder phone call prior to the session.

Questions
_____ Questions should flow in a logical sequence.
_____ Key questions should focus on the critical issues.
_____ Use probe or follow-up questions as needed.
_____ Limit the use of "why" questions.
_____ Use "think-back" questions as needed.

Logistics
_____ The room should be satisfactory (size, tables, comfort, sound, etc.).
_____ Arrive early.
_____ Check background noise so it doesn't interfere with tape recording.
_____ Have name tents for participants.
_____ Place a remote microphone on the table.
_____ Place the tape recorder off the table near the assistant moderator's chair.
_____ Bring extra tapes, batteries, and extension cords.
_____ Plan topics for small-talk conversation.
_____ Seat experts and talkative participants next to the moderator.
_____ Seat shy and quiet participants directly across from moderator.
_____ Serve food.
_____ Bring enough copies of handouts and/or visual aids.

Moderator Skills
_____ Practice introduction without referring to notes.
_____ Practice questions. Know the key questions. Be aware of timing.
_____ Be well rested and alert.
_____ Listen. Are participants answering the question?
_____ Know when to probe for more information and when to move on.
_____ Avoid head nodding.
_____ Avoid verbal comments that signal approval.
_____ Avoid giving personal opinions.

Immediately After the Session
_____ Check to see if the tape recorder captured the comments.
_____ Debrief with the research team.
_____ Prepare a brief written summary of key points as soon as possible.

Practice Hint 5.2
Responsibilities of Assistant Moderators

1. *Take responsibility for all equipment and supplies. Make sure you have enough of all the items needed.*

> Tape recorder
> Microphone
> Extension cords (power and microphone)
> Blank tapes
> Name tents (5-by-8-inch index cards)
> Incentives and receipt form
> Markers, pens, pencils, crayons, paper
> Refreshments
> Duct tape to hold down the cords
> Spare batteries
> Visuals or handouts

2. *Take responsibility for refreshments.* Arrange for the refreshments and set them up in the room.

3. *Arrange the room.* Arrange chairs and table so everyone can see each other. Be attentive to background noises that would affect the audio recording.

4. *Set up the equipment.* Verify that it is working properly.

5. *Welcome participants as they arrive.*

6. *Sit in a designated location.* Sit outside the circle, opposite the moderator, and close to the door. If someone arrives after the session begins, meet the person at the door, take him or her outside of the room, and give him or her a short briefing as to what has happened and the current topic of discussion. Then bring the late participant into the room and show him or her where to sit.

7. *Take notes throughout the discussion.* Be attentive to the following areas of concern.

   - Well-said quotes. Capture word for word. Listen for sentences or phrases that are particularly enlightening or eloquently express a particular point of view. Place quotation marks around the statement or phrase and indicate name of speaker. Place your opinions, thoughts, or ideas in parentheses to keep them separate from participant comments.

   - If a question occurs to you that you would like to ask at the end of the discussion, write it down in a circle or box.

   - Note the nonverbal activity. Watch for the obvious, such as head nods, physical excitement, eye contact between certain participants, or other clues that would indicate level of agreement, support, or interest.

   - Make a sketch of the seating arrangement.

8. *Monitor recording equipment.* Occasionally glance at the tape recorder to see if the reels are moving. Turn over the tape or insert another tape when appropriate. Attempt to do this as smoothly as possible without drawing attention to the recording equipment. Label the cassette tapes. Indicate date, location, and number of each tape.

9. *Do not participate in the discussion!* You can talk only if invited by the moderator. Control your nonverbal actions no matter how strongly you feel about an issue.

10. *Ask questions when invited.* At the end of the discussion, the moderator will invite you to ask questions of amplification or clarification.

11. *Give an oral summary.* At the end of the discussion, the moderator or assistant should provide a brief summary (about two minutes) of responses to the important questions. Invite participants to offer additions or corrections to the summary.

12. *Hand out the incentives.* Have participants sign a receipt form for the incentive if necessary. Thank the participants for attending.

13. *Debrief.* Following the focus group, participate in the debriefing with the moderator. Record the debriefing.

14. *Provide feedback on analysis.* Read and provide feedback on the analysis.

Practice Hint 5.3:
Tips on Using Money as an Incentive

Financial incentives are standard in market research focus groups, but they can present challenges for public and nonprofit organizations. Public institutions often find it difficult, if not impossible, to give out cash incentives to focus group participants. An accountant at a large university told us that the university could not give money because there was no precedent and no category for it in the accounting procedures. When you think about it, public institutions rarely pay in cash. If you are granted authorization to use cash, be sure to use sound fiscal procedures that ensure protection of monies. Here are some suggestions:

1. The focus group participants who receive cash incentives should sign a receipt that they have received payment. In addition, you might ask participants for some type of identifying number or address.

2. The moderator who takes the money into the field should be expected to "sign" for the money before going on the road and then, when the groups are concluded, to produce receipts of money given out plus unused cash totaling the amount received.

3. Envelopes containing cash are prepared before the group. One envelope is prepared for each participant. It has the participant's name on the outside and their cash inside the sealed envelope.

4. The cash incentives are carried in a secure manner.

5. Each person in the focus group should receive the same amount of money. Never pay someone more or less than another participant.

6. The moderator or assistant moderator distributes the incentives and gets participants to sign the receipt at the end of the focus group.

Remember, there will come a time when it is inappropriate, awkward, or impossible to use money as an incentive. The old rule is, if you don't have money, you do need creativity. With creativity you may come up with incentives that are even better than money.

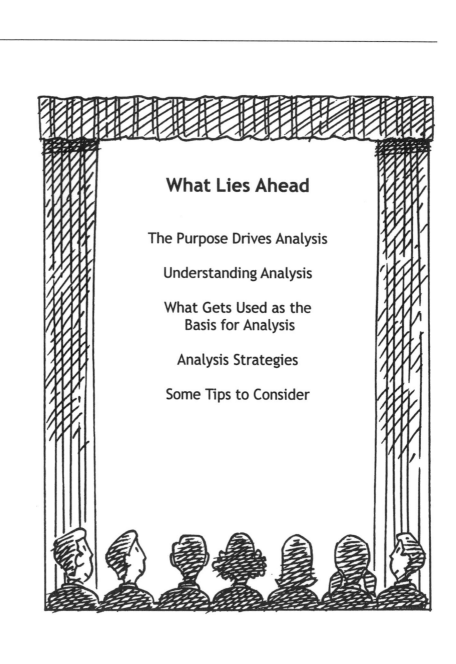

6

Analyzing Focus Group Results

A statement of what data analysis is:

> Data analysis consists of examining, categorizing, tabulating, or otherwise recombining the evidence, to address the initial propositions of a study. (Yin, 1984, p. 99)

A story of what data analysis is not:

Once upon a time, an institution of higher learning set out to hire a new president. The governing board of the institution sought applications from far and near, but because of the limited travel budget, only the near applications were seriously considered. It turned out that three professors were among the final candidates to be interviewed by the board. The first was a professor of accounting, the second was a professor of engineering, and the third was a professor who regularly served as a management consultant. After completing all interviews, the board was deadlocked. In an attempt to resolve the dilemma, the board decided to invite all three professors back to answer one final question.

The accounting professor was the first to be asked, "What is two plus two?"

The professor immediately replied, "With great confidence, I can tell you that the answer is exactly four."

The engineering professor was the second candidate to be asked, "What is two plus two?"

After a moment of reflection, the engineer replied, "In the field of engineering, we are accustomed to problems such as this. In engineering we frequently must deal with numbers that are rounded. Therefore, the first two could be any number between 1.50 and 2.49, and the same is true of the second number. This means that the sum of two plus two could be any number between 3.00 and 4.98."

Finally the board invited the management consultant into the board-room. The question was asked, "What is two plus two?"

The consultant slowly got up and went over to shut the door, then over to the window to close the blinds, and finally back to the board table. The consultant leaned across the table and, with a voice slightly over a whisper, asked, "What do you want it to be?"

Qualitative analysis is not whatever you want it to be, but unfortunately, that is a perception that is sometimes held. The intent of this chapter is to present an overview of focus group analysis—analysis that is practical, systematic, and verifiable.

Analysis can be a stumbling block for qualitative researchers. The unanticipated volume of data is sobering, but more often it is the complexity of the analysis that stops the researcher cold.

The Purpose Drives Analysis

Analysis begins by going back to the intent of the study. Indeed, throughout the analysis process, the researcher should remember the purpose of the study. Qualitative researchers have been known to be overwhelmed with the vast accumulation of data and find that they have a multitude of choices. A key principle is that the depth or intensity of analysis is determined by the purpose of the study. At times, the purpose of the study is narrow, and elaborate analysis isn't needed or appropriate. Difficulties emerge in both qualitative and quantitative analysis when there is a mismatch between analysis resources and the problem. This can result in elaborate analysis of trivial data or inadequate analysis of a complex problem of major concern. The researcher must remember the intent of the study and regularly weigh choices against two factors: available resources and the value of that new information.

In some respects, beginning the focus group analysis is like standing at the entrance of a maze. Several different paths are readily apparent at the beginning, and as the traveler continues, additional paths and choices continually emerge. It is unknown to the traveler if the path will be productive until it has been explored, but the process of exploration requires an investment of effort even if it is just a peek

BACKGROUND

Purpose, Purpose, Purpose

This is the analysis chapter, so we just wanted to know if you've picked up on this theme. We keep pointing to purpose. That's because the purpose keeps us on track. If we are clear about it all along the way, we are more efficient and effective at getting the needed information. The purpose influences everything. It drives the planning. It suggests how much time and resources should be put into the study. It gives us clues as to what type of people should be recruited to participate. It guides the development of the questions. It helps the moderator know what to focus on. And it helps the analyst(s) know what to focus on. We emphasize this because beginning researchers sometimes get so excited about all the different things they could learn from a study or all the fascinating things that are said in focus groups that they get lost. Our focus on purpose doesn't mean we aren't open to different things. We don't put blinders on. But we know when we are looking at something beyond the purpose, and we weigh the potential benefit of exploring it.

around the corner. Survival requires a clear fix on the purpose of the study.

Understanding Analysis

Focus group analysis is systematic, sequential, verifiable, and continuous.

Analysis Is Systematic and Sequential

Systematic analysis is deliberate and planned—not capricious, arbitrary, or spontaneous. Analysis is a sequential, evolving process. Systematic, sequential analysis procedures help ensure that results will reflect what was shared in the groups. We institute systematic protocol to avoid making mistakes or overlooking critical factors. Systematic analysis means that the analysis strategy is documented, understood, and able to be clearly articulated by each member of the research team. You are ready for the question, "How did you come up with that?" and can point to the trail of evidence at the drop of a hat. The process is open for inspection.

Analysis Is Verifiable

Another researcher should be able to arrive at similar conclusions using available documents and the data. As humans, there is a tendency to selectively see or hear those comments that confirm a particular point of view or to avoid dealing with information that causes us dissonance or that we don't understand. Our training, our background, and our experiences influence what we notice and what we attend to. Researchers must continually be careful to avoid the trap of selective perception. Verification in analysis is a critical safeguard.

For analysis to be verifiable, there must be sufficient data to constitute a trail of evidence. The data stream begins with field notes and recordings taken during each focus group, continues with the oral summary (verification) of key points during each group, goes into the debriefing with the moderator team immediately following the groups, and includes transcripts if used.

Analysis Is a Continuing Process

Focus group analysis is quite different from analysis of numbers. One distinct difference is when analysis begins and ends. When analyzing numbers, researchers often wait until all forms, surveys, or documents are obtained. When everything is available, or at least a reasonable amount is available, the data entry begins. Codes are identified, and the raw data are entered into the computer. Data collection stops, and analysis begins. The separation between collection and analysis is clear in quantitative studies. By contrast, focus group analysis begins earlier—in the first focus group. Focus group analysis is done concurrently with data collection. Each subsequent group is analyzed and compared to earlier groups.

In fact, doing analysis as you go improves data collection. Beginning moderators should consider scheduling focus groups so they have time to transcribe the tape from one group before conducting the next. Also try to write a short summary of the group, going question by question. You will spot whether you need to get more information on a particular question. You will see where the group didn't really answer the question, so you can be alert to that in the next group. You can spot a question that isn't really getting at the type of information the client needs and adapt the question in later groups. Analyzing along the way makes the moderator better.

Setting the Stage for Analysis

A foundation is laid before the first focus group is conducted. It begins with the moderator or analyst becoming familiar with the area of study, obtaining background data about the problem, exploring past research, and discussing the project with the client or sponsor. Then the study design begins to emerge by making decisions about the needed qualities of focus group participants. Groups must be configured in a way to allow for the type of analysis wanted. Again, if you want to analyze how women versus men feel, they must be in different groups. The questions must be written in ways that allow for analysis. Even before the first group begins, the moderator or analyst carefully reviews the set of questions and reflects on how these questions meet the research specifications and yield insights. Probes are anticipated, and clarification is sought when participant responses are trivial or superficial.

The sequential process continues during the group and, in fact, becomes a critical part of the focus group. The questions are sequentially arranged, and later comments by participants build on earlier comments within the group. Early questions are often of minimal importance and may get limited attention in analysis (or sometimes are even set aside). However, the responses to later questions are typically critical to the study. Strategically placed ending questions (see Chapter

3) help nail down the main points of participants, and a short verbal summary (Chapter 4) at the conclusion of the discussion allows for verification.

The sequence continues after the focus group with an immediate debriefing with the moderator and assistant moderator and can also include other members of the research team who have observed the session. At this time, the moderator makes a quick check to ensure that the tape recorder worked and that the field notes are complete. Then the moderator turns the tape recorder back on, and the team members discuss what they heard: What were the themes? What were the particularly helpful quotes? What was surprising? How was this group similar to or different from earlier groups? Does anything need to be changed before the next group?

The sequence continues but may take a number of different paths from here. The paths are described later in this chapter under "Analysis Strategies."

What Gets Used as the Basis for Analysis

Depending on the purpose of the study, the time line, the budget, and the needs of the client, different ways of capturing the data are used as the basis for analysis: transcripts, tapes, notes, and memory.

Transcript Based

Transcript-based analysis uses unabridged transcripts of the focus groups as a basis for analysis. These are often supplemented with field notes taken by researchers. Soon after the focus group, the researcher or a typist completes the transcript, which can easily be thirty to fifty pages of single-spaced text. In the hands of a speedy typist with proper equipment, the transcript of a two-hour focus group can require from eight to twelve hours to prepare. This transcript is normally single-spaced with double spacing between different speakers. Whatever is said by the moderator is capitalized or bolded for easy spotting.

With the transcript, the researcher has several options, some of which are described later (long table or coding via computer). Normally the analyst reads the transcript and makes notes, codes sections, or develops categories. Often the transcripts are printed with a wide margin, allowing for notes and comments to be added in the analysis stage. Some analysts use colored marking pens or scissors to cut out or identify sections of interest or relevance to the study.

The analyst then prepares a report that summarizes the findings and compares and contrasts the findings from different audience groups in the study. The report may be prepared using the focus group questions as an outline or by themes if the themes tend to cut across questions.

Tape Based—Abridged Transcript

Tape-based analysis is slightly less time-consuming than the transcript-based strategy. The tape-based approach relies on listening to a tape recording of each focus group and then developing an abridged transcript of the relevant and useful portions of the discussion. Instead of a thirty- to fifty-page complete transcript, the abridged transcript might consist of only fifteen to thirty pages. It is a condensed version of the focus group with irrelevant conversation removed.

Only someone with a thorough understanding of the purpose of the study can develop an abridged transcript. Some conversation may seem irrelevant or redundant to those not familiar with the study or research. Or they may think it is like taking minutes of a meeting (it isn't). This abridged transcript should be prepared by a member of the research team.

Note Based

Note-based analysis relies mainly on field notes. The focus group also might have been audio or video recorded, but these sources are used only as a backup or if there is a need for clarifying the notes. The great advantage of the note-based analysis is speed.

The quality of the note-based approach is directly related to the ability of the assistant moderator to capture relevant notes. The moderator's notes, by contrast, are typically sketchy and incomplete because of the need for concentrating on the discussion. Consistency is needed in note taking because in some situations, the moderator will be doing the analysis based on the assistant moderator's notes. In all cases, the notes should indicate when something was a direct quote or when the note taker has paraphrased the participant's comments.

Memory Based

Memory-based analysis is best left to professionals. It requires considerable skill and experience and has substantial potential for error in the hands of a novice. This type of analysis is regularly used by professional moderators in the special focus group rooms with one-way mirrors. After the focus group, the moderator goes around to the back room and offers a memory-based summary of the critical points. The moderator may have made a few sketchy notes, but the summary is largely from memory.

This type of analysis unquestionably lends itself to those studies in which the results are rather clear-cut such as a choice between products and the potential success of a new product. The strategy also works better when the focus group questions are concrete, when the moderator requests a specific response from each participant, and when the moderator uses a flip chart or more detailed notes to capture key points.

The report is oral and allows time for questions and reflections from the clients who watched the focus group. Veteran moderators find that they may need to dislodge unfounded conclusions or interpretations developed by the sponsors who were watching the group. There is a tendency for sponsors to find support for their preexisting convictions, and the role of the moderator-analyst is to guide them out of these traps with a balanced perspective.

Analysis Strategies

This is where people get stuck. They wonder what to do with all those transcripts, tapes, and notes. It can be overwhelming. We suggest beginning analysts use the long-table approach. It is a time-tested method and breaks down the process into manageable chunks.

Long-Table Approach

The long-table approach is a low-technology option that has been used in countless analysis projects. It allows the analyst to identify themes and categorize results. It isn't an elegant or sophisticated-looking strategy, but it works. This is what you need:

- A room where you can spread out your work and it can remain undisturbed until you are done with analysis. It helps to have a long table(s). Lots of floor space will substitute nicely, if you don't mind bending down and you can keep the kids and dogs out of the area. Walls work too if you don't mind taping things to them.
- Transcripts

- Scissors
- Colored marking pens
- Colored paper for copying the transcripts
- Flip chart or newsprint paper

You are going to cut the transcripts apart. But once they are cut into individual quotes, you will also want to know where the quote came from originally. Here are a couple of tips that can help you identify where quotes came from after your transcripts are cut into hundreds of little pieces.

Tip 1: Number each line of each transcript. Most word-processing software has a feature that will do this for you. The line numbers will help you quickly locate a quote within a transcript.

Tip 2: Print transcripts on different colors of paper, thereby color coding the transcripts by audience type, category, and so on (e.g., student groups on blue, parent groups on green, etc.). Or run a blue marking pen down the left margin of each page of student groups and a green marker down the left margin of each page of the parent transcripts. (Or if you want to be even more systematic, give the first student group one blue line, the second two blue lines, and the third three blue lines. That way, you can not only tell student groups from the parent groups, but you can also tell which student group it came from.) This helps you know where quotes came from after you have cut the transcripts apart.

Make two hard copies of each transcript, one to cut up (the working transcript) and one that stays intact. Put the transcripts that are to stay intact in your files.

Arrange the working transcripts in a reasonable order. It could be in the sequence in which the groups were conducted, but more likely, it will be by categories of participants or by some demographic screening characteristics of participants. For example, if you did three groups with students, three groups with parents, and three groups with teachers, you would work with all three transcripts of one kind (e.g., students) before moving to the next. This arrangement helps you be alert to changes that may be occurring from one type of audience group to another.

Before cutting, do a quick reading of all transcripts. This quick reading is just to remind you of the whole scope and to refresh your memory of what was said in the groups.

Place the flip chart or newsprint paper on long tables, on the floor, or on the walls. Write one of the focus group questions to be analyzed on the top of each page of newsprint. If you had ten questions to analyze, you now have ten pages of newsprint surrounding you. You may also want to divide the newsprint page into categories to represent different types of focus group participants. For example, on one part of the page you could place comments from student focus groups, in another location you could place comments from parent focus groups, and in a third section you could place comments from teacher focus groups.

Now it's time to begin the cutting and categorizing.

Read each quote and answer these questions:

Point 1. Did the participant answer the question that was asked?
— IF YES go to Point 3.
— DON'T KNOW set it aside and review it later.
— IF NO go to Point 2.

(If you are undecided or unclear about any answers, then take the conservative approach and save the comments and review them later.)

Point 2. Does the comment answer a different question in the focus group?
— IF YES move it to appropriate question.
— IF NO go to Point 3.

(Caution: Don't assume that answers will follow the questions. Occasionally, participants will provide answers to questions asked earlier or to questions that have not yet been asked. When this occurs, move the comment to the appropriate location.)

Point 3. Does the comment say something of importance about the topic?
— IF YES tape it to the newsprint under the appropriate question.
— IF NO set it aside.

Tip: Don't use a lot of tape because you will want to move the quotes around later.

Point 4. Is it like something that has been said earlier?
— IF YES start grouping like quotes together. You are basically making piles (categories) of like things.
— IF NO start a separate pile.

You are constantly comparing and making decisions. Is this similar to or different from other things?

Soon the newsprint page is filling up with participant quotes. Not everything necessarily fits neatly into categories. In focus groups, people regularly get off topic or expand in detail on an aspect of minimal importance to the study. There's a good chance that you won't use this information, and you will want to set it aside to clear the clutter, but don't toss these out. Instead, create storage areas so you can later review these quotes again. You might rearrange categories or create new categories and want to review these unused quotes to see if they fit your new categories. Sometimes the storage area is a box in the middle of the room with unused quotes.

After you've completed cutting up all the transcripts, you're ready to begin analysis of specific questions. Make sure you have all the quotes that say similar things together. Rearrange until you're satisfied. You may want to talk with someone else about how you are categorizing certain things. Or you may want to show them. When you finish putting quotes into categories, you are ready for the next step.

Go back to each newsprint page and write a descriptive summary of what each type of group said in response to the question. Write a description of what students said in response to the question. Then write a summary for the parents and then the teachers. Again, you are comparing and contrasting. How are they similar? How are they different? At this point, just describe what was said. Later you may want to go further and offer an interpretation of what it means or a recommendation.

During this process, you will need to decide how much weight or emphasis to give comments or themes. We look at several factors:

Frequency. Although we pay attention to how frequently something is said, it is a huge mistake to assume that what is said most frequently is most important. Sometimes a really key insight might have been said only once in a series of groups. You have to know enough about what you are studying to spot a gem when it comes along.

Specificity. Typically, we give more emphasis to comments that are specific—that provide detail. For example, if we were asking what people dislike about flying, we would give more weight to a quote that specifically described a time when that person lost his or her bags, what he or she did, and what happened than to a comment of "Oh, I hate it when they lose your bags."

Emotion. Also, we typically give more weight to comments or themes in which participants show emotion, enthusiasm, passion, or intensity in their answers.

Extensiveness. Frequency and extensiveness are related but different. Extensiveness is how many different people said something. Frequency is how many times something is said. We have had groups in which one person kept returning to the same theme. Although the theme was mentioned a fair amount, it was brought up by only one person. We pay attention to extensiveness.

When you are done writing a descriptive summary for each of the questions, look across the questions to see what themes cut across the questions. Are there things that come up repeatedly? If so, consider structuring your written report around these themes rather than around the questions. Or perhaps some questions can be combined.

Now take a break. Get away from the data for a couple of days. This is a chance to refocus your attention on the big picture. What prompted the study? Who's going to use the results, and have you located the information that will be helpful? How can you frame this information so it best conveys what participants shared? It's easy to get sidetracked by fascinating tidbits of minor importance. After a few days, go back to conclude the analysis.

When we write a report, we structure it around the questions or the themes. Then we use the summaries we wrote earlier to describe what was said about the question or the theme. If we are writing a narrative report, we then select quotes from those categories that illustrate what was said. The quotes are used as evidence. We look for quotes that capture the essence of what was said. They give the reader an idea of how the participants talked. We typically use about three quotes per category or theme.

When we have completed this level of analysis, then we may go on to include our interpretations or recommendations. However, we are careful to keep these sections separate from the findings section that we just completed through the process outlined above.

The long-table approach has been around a long time, but it is still effective. Quite a number of variations are possible, but the core elements are basically cutting, sorting, and arranging through comparing and contrasting.

We recommend that people who are doing their first qualitative analysis project use this process. It is systematic. It breaks the job down into doable chunks. It helps make analysis a visual process. Once you have mastered this approach to analysis, you have a better idea of how to adapt the process to meet the needs of other efforts.

Using the Computer to Help Manage the Data

Computers have been used in a variety of ways in focus group analysis. We are aware of three distinct approaches, but likely more exist. For each approach, it is assumed that you have transcripts.

One approach is simply using the word processor as another way to cut and paste. Essentially, it is using the computer to perform the long-table analysis described earlier. When used in this way, give thought to the need for tracing the source of each quote. It's easy to block and paste quotes together and then lose sight of where they came from. Sometimes knowing the source is critical. This can be solved by developing a coding system that allows you to identify each quote by group and/or participant.

A second approach is to go beyond cutting and pasting functions of word-processing programs and begin to code quotes. A number of researchers have been creative with the use of sorting, coding, and macros. Essentially, they use the capabilities of software they already use to analyze the results. This system may not be as elegant as the specialized software, but it has benefit because the researchers are already familiar with the software.

The third approach is to use the specially developed software that is designed for qualitative analysis. Two popular programs are The Ethnograph and NUD*IST. These programs open the doors for analysis possibilities that are not reasonable with other strategies. For example, these programs allow you to "nest" codes. This means that you might have a shorter quote within a longer quote, and each one can be coded differently. Earlier procedures tended to limit you to placing quotes in one location, but with these special computer programs, there is no limit. Or you might want to examine comments from participants with certain demographic characteristics that you've coded into your computer. It can be done with other analysis strategies, but it is difficult and awkward.

The advantage of these specially developed computer programs is that they help manage large sets of text. It helps an analyst look very carefully at the data. As a result, these programs are popular in academic settings, particularly graduate research. The downside is the time needed to learn and operate the program. Also, they provide a level of analysis not always needed.

Rapid Approach

Sometimes speed is a critical concern. Perhaps a decision is about to be made and rapid results are critical. Caution is always advised when speed is a driving force. When speed is urgent, veteran moderators often use several strategies, such as the following:

- Tightly focus the study
- Carefully develop the questions to foster fast analysis
- Ask fewer questions than normal
- Use flip charts to capture comments
- Give oral summaries at the end of the groups
- Use assistant moderators to provide verification

Sound Approach

This is an innovative approach that is made possible by equipment and software that allow for digitally recording the focus group. With specialized software (Sound Forge is an example), the moderator can record sound on the laptop computer and mark certain segments that show usefulness for later analysis. Then the researcher can quickly go back over the transcript, find the marker, locate the actual quote, and play back the quote. Later the quotes can be clustered, just as you would cluster written quotes, and you can embed the actual comments on reports that are prepared on CD disks. Note the article by Pierre Belisle (1998, p. 18) in *Quirk's Marketing Research Review*.

BACKGROUND

If you would like to read more about the Rapid Focus Group, check out Chapter 12 in:

Krueger, R. A. (1998). *Moderating Focus Groups*. Thousand Oaks, CA: Sage.

Some Tips to Consider

Let's cut to the chase. Suppose that in the near future, you have to analyze a series of focus groups. What would be the most valuable advice that we could offer? We suggest the following.

Know What Is Needed in Your Research Environment

The approaches to focus group research can vary greatly, and one form of analysis can be completely impractical or be disregarded in your setting. Find out how previous analysis was done. If this is the first time you've analyzed focus groups, seek advice from colleagues about how other research has been conducted. Analysis for a dissertation is a world apart from analysis for a small, nonprofit agency with a shoe-string budget.

Being There Is Best

Nothing beats being present in the focus group. We highly encourage that analysis be done by someone who was physically present in the room when the focus group was conducted. It's been estimated that 80% of the content is found in the transcript, and the remaining 20% are all the other things that occur in the room. In some groups, the environment must be sensed and felt.

Not Everything Is Worthy of Analysis or Can Be Analyzed

Beginning analysts often make the mistake of assuming that they must use all the data. In some focus groups, much of the discussion may be of marginal value, but in other groups, the comments are rich and insightful. Certain questions are more important than others, and you must know one from the other. Place your attention on parts of the group discussion in which the most relevant conversation is being held.

Analysis Is Based on Pattern Identification

An elementary teacher had an interesting way of teaching classification systems. The teacher would bring out a large box full of keys and dump the keys in the center of the room. The teacher told students to arrange the keys. The students would ask questions about how they might do

it. The teacher said that there could be many ways, and they should think about it and then place the keys in categories. The kids eagerly got into the task, discussing possibilities, comparing strategies, changing directions several times, and then finally coming to agreement about a preferred method. Sometimes they would abandon one method and use something different. It was always an interesting exercise. Some kids would sort the keys by color or metal (brass, iron, and nickel); others would sort by size (small, medium, large); and still others would sort by the key type (automotive, house, padlock, luggage, etc.). There were no wrong ways to do it, and after a while, a student would ask about the purposes of classification systems. (The teachable moment!) Was it to arrange keys for future use? Was it for an aesthetic display? The way we categorize depends on our purpose. In a similar way, focus group researchers must reflect on the purpose of their categories. These categories are often determined by the purpose of the study.

Beware of Personal Bias or Preexisting Opinions About the Topic

People differ in how they analyze. Some have hunches about what they might find, and when they find the first evidence that confirms that hunch, they leap to conclusions. Sometimes the leap is premature. Always challenge yourself before you leap. Seek evidence that disproves or presents counterinformation. Seek insight from colleagues, particularly those with different backgrounds. Be ready to release your grip on an interpretation and embrace alternatives. Preexisting opinions can sometimes be helpful, but they can also be dangerous. Be open to multiple realities.

You Are the Voice of the Participants

Consider yourself the voice or interpreter of the participants. Your task is to clearly communicate how participants felt about the topic. In a way, you are their spokesperson. There may be different voices and multiple views that need to be presented, and your task is to accurately represent the range of views.

Visual Representation of Reality

Give thought to drawing a picture of your findings. Sometimes flow charts, matrices, diagrams, and so on are helpful in depicting results. Other times, sketches, drawings, images, cartoons, or analogies are helpful. Anselm Strauss (1988) uses visual techniques to help students with qualitative analysis. The visual representation is helpful both in forming the analysis and later when results are communicated.

Leave the Numbers Out

We pay attention to frequency, but we don't count things up, and we rarely include numbers in reports. Numbers are misleading in focus group reports. Readers often want to turn numbers into percentages and project to the population. This is unwise. The sample size is too small. Not everyone answers every question. Some people may comment three times on one issue. Other people may not comment at all. Instead, use modifiers such as *no one, a few, some, many, most,* or *all* to describe how many people talked about an issue in a particular way.

SUMMARY

Focus group analysis is a deliberate, purposeful process. It is systematic, uses verifiable procedures, is done in a sequential manner, and is a continuing process. Many analysis strategies can be used, yet each pays attention to the critical qualities. Transcripts, audiotapes, and notes are used as the basis for analysis. Try the long-table approach as a way of making analysis concrete. Computers can also be helpful. For those who face the prospect of doing focus group analysis in the near future, we offer some tips to make the task more manageable.

Practice Hint 6.1
Transcribing Focus Groups

Transcribing Focus Group Interviews

Here are some suggestions if you are considering transcribing focus group interviews:

1. *Identify moderator statements.* Always identify the comments of the moderator. Use a consistent style such as bolding, capitalizations, or underlining.

2. *Use a consistent style.* Single-space all comments. Double-space between speakers. Number all pages. Place a header on all pages indicating date and group name.

3. *Don't worry about punctuation.* People don't speak in complete sentences. Use punctuation where it seems to make sense. Place periods at what seem to be the end of sentences. Do a spell check. Check with the client for concerns about spelling of technical words, jargon, and acronyms. Some won't worry about the spelling of those internal words. Others will want them spelled right.

4. *Don't type verbal pauses such as "umms" or "ahs."*

5. *Type comments word for word.* This is a transcript, not minutes of a meeting. The conversation is recorded word for word. Don't change the words or correct the grammar. If some of the words are unintelligible, then type three periods . . . to indicate that words are missing from the transcript.

6. *Note special or unusual sounds that could help analysis.* Use parentheses to indicate laughter, loud voices, shouting, or someone being interrupted.

7. *Allow sufficient time.* Typically, it takes about four to eight hours to type one hour of tape. But the time will vary with typist speed, the quality of the tape recording, the length of the session, the experience of the typist with focus groups, and the complexity of the topic.

8. *Use quality playback equipment.* The typist should avoid tape players with small speakers and awkward buttons. Consider earphones. Focus group interview tapes *always* have background noise, and participants will speak with different tones and voice levels—therefore, these tapes will require concentration and the best quality playback equipment that can be obtained. If possible, use equipment with a tape speed control and foot-operated backspace.

9. *Minimize distractions.* Type transcripts in a place with minimal distractions or interruptions.

10. *Questions to ask the researcher before beginning the transcription.* Here are some topics that should be clarified before having someone transcribe the focus group tapes:

    a. Did the researcher make a backup tape?

    b. Should the introduction be transcribed?

    c. Should the debriefing with the research team following the focus group be transcribed?

d. Did anything special occur in the group that is of particular interest?

e. What should be done with informal comments from one person to another that are captured on tape but not part of the formal focus group?

f. Should an effort be made to identify names of participants? (Give the transcriptionist a sketch of the seating pattern.)

g. If there are technical problems with the recording, what should the transcriptionist do? Call for instructions? Note the problem in the transcript and continue transcribing? Other?

h. What do you do when voices suddenly become faint or hard to hear?

i. What do you do when several people are talking at once?

j. How does the client want to get the transcript? Hard copy? Disk copy? Through e-mail? In what type of word-processing program?

k. Does the client want to receive the transcripts as they are completed or all at once?

Contracting With a Transcriptionist

Contracting with a transcriptionist can be difficult. From the transcriptionist's perspective, an hourly basis is often preferred because of the variety of sound quality and differences in groups. Some tapes just require more time than others. From the researcher's perspective, it is difficult to manage a budget without knowing the total cost of transcribing. Transcriptionists can vary in speed and quality. Researchers often prefer a fixed amount per tape. Use the first transcription as a test to determine cost and level of accuracy.

The Future of Transcription

Soon, a breakthrough will occur with voice recognition software that will change the nature of computer analysis. Voice recognition software allows you to talk to your computer, and the computer immediately transcribes what you've said. (It's the stuff you've seen on *Star Trek* 30 years ago, when Scotty just goes to the computer and asks a question and gets an answer.) The breakthrough will occur when these programs become capable of recognizing different voices and correctly identify the voice of the speaker. At present, these programs need to be "trained" to recognize your voice, and when someone else speaks, it looks like gibberish. That will change, and we will have instantaneous transcriptions.

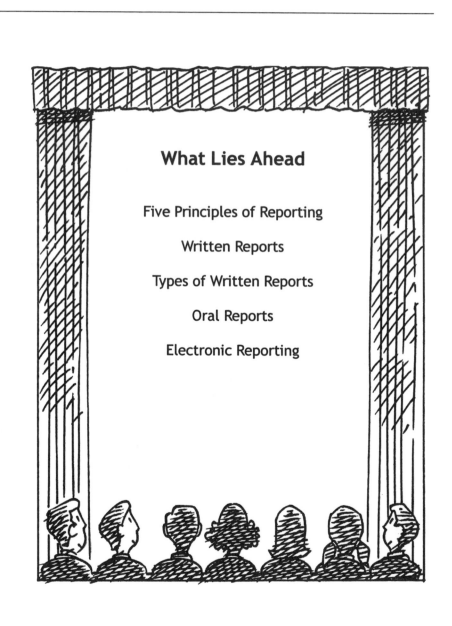

7
Reporting

Five Principles of Reporting

Five principles serve as the foundation of reporting. Later we'll refer to these in differing ways, but here we'll be very explicit. Everything else in this chapter builds on these points. The points are as follows.

Know the Point and Get to It Quickly

No matter what type of report—written or spoken, formal or informal, one-to-one or to a large group—always know the point and get to it quickly. Everything in the report should have a purpose. If it doesn't have a clear purpose, take it out.

Clear, Effective Writing Takes Time

In 1657, Pascal wrote, "I have made this letter longer than usual, only because I have not had the time to make it shorter." Clarity and crispness take effort.

Provide Enlightenment

The primary purpose of a report is to enlighten someone—to bring knowledge, help understand feelings, or convey information. Ask yourself, "What do I have that is new, important, or valuable to my audience?" The best reporters spend time considering what may be enlightening to their readers.

Involve People Throughout the Study

In the public and nonprofit environment, focus groups that involve people throughout the study tend to produce results. Involve the end users in conducting the study—in planning, recruiting, moderating, analyzing, or reporting aspects of the focus group study. The benefit is clear. If you want people to actually use the results of the study, make it their study instead of your study.

Use Multiple Reporting Strategies

Researchers often assume that other people like to get information in the same way they like to get information. But people have different preferred learning styles. In addition, a few of us will get the message the first time, but most of us need reinforcement and reminders. Successful reporting uses multiple methods such as one-to-one, oral briefings, written reports, presentations, media reports, or reports presented by a variety of people. These reports can be complemented with audio and/or visuals—charts, photographs, audio- or videotapes, drawings made by focus group participants, and diagrams. Reports using multiple media help ensure that the message is effectively communicated. The combination of methods accommodates individual learning preferences and reinforces findings.

Written Reports

People have better ways to spend their time than laboring over dry, confusing reports. At least we do. We are constantly trying to learn how to better communicate ideas. We've picked up these tips from colleagues, and we use many of these ourselves. Try them.

Study Popular Writing

Study popular news magazines. Notice how the writing flows and entices the reader to continue. Note how boxes, sidebars, and visuals help convey the messages. Consider what strategies you can use in your writing.

Realistically Assess Your Own Ability

When was the last time you had a professional help you with your writing? Take a refresher class. Seek out a group to give you feedback.

Consider finding a personal coach. At a minimum, use the computer to get an estimate of the reading level of your text.

Find What Helps You Write

Preferences and styles vary greatly. Some people thrive as deadlines zoom closer. Others crumble. Some writers have a special time of day when words leap out. Some have a special place. Some write from outlines and others from inspiration. A few can write anytime, anywhere, under any conditions.

Little goals help us write. They make the task seem doable. Then we give ourselves little rewards. Like, "I have to write three pages a day until this is done. After three pages I can do anything I want." Or, "If I write for four hours I'll take a motorcycle ride." Often we exceed our little goals because once we get going it seems easy. The little goals and rewards get us started. It's a lot easier to face writing three pages today than it is to think about writing a whole report, article, chapter, or book. Those feel overwhelming. "It will take forever, and I will never get to see sunlight again." However, "Three pages? No problem. I'll see sunlight this afternoon!" Reflect on what helps you write. If something isn't working, try a different approach.

Edit Ruthlessly and Plan for Multiple Revisions

Never assume that the first draft will be your final draft. In fact, let your first draft be crummy. Just get it down. Then edit. Quality writing comes from feedback loops. Build in these loops from the beginning, allow time in the schedule for feedback, and seek out constructive comments.

Dazzle With Your Ideas— Not With Fancy Words

Some writers use complex, arcane language instead of clear, straightforward prose. The ideas, the concepts, and the findings should not be overshadowed by showy language. (Incidentally, the parallel in the oral report is when something about the speaker draws attention away from the content.) In focus groups we phrase questions using the words the people in the group would use to talk about a topic. Consider doing the same thing with the report. When conveying the results, use language the audience would use. Your goal is to communicate to others. Make your report easy for them to understand.

Make the Report Visually Attractive

Whether we like it or not, books are sometimes judged by their covers. The look and feel of the written report are important. Does it look professional? Does it look like care and attention went into the document? Is it designed to keep the readers' attention? Does it guide their eyes over the document? Seek professional help in design, take a class to improve your skills, or, if nothing else, keep a file of attractive, well-designed reports to serve as models.

Types of Written Reports

Focus group reports traditionally have been presented in a narrative style. Alternatives include the report memo, the top-line report, and the bulleted report. Let's review the key ingredients of each of these.

Narrative Report

The narrative report is recognized by its length and use of quotations. Typically, these reports are between fifteen and thirty pages long, but occasionally, a report might become lengthy, reaching close to one hundred pages. The danger of excessive length is that it limits readability, except for the most interested and ardent client.

Top-Line Report

The top-line report conveys the critical points in the most economical manner. These brief bulleted reports are prepared primarily with field notes and moderator memory and are presented back to the client within a day or two of the focus group. These reports are also called top-of-mind reports, which is actually more descriptive of the process. Top-line reports are oriented toward the particular decision or problem that gave rise to the focus group. As a result, this report won't contain information unless it is specifically relevant to the purpose of the study. The top-line report is usually an interim or preliminary report that is prepared quickly and provides immediate findings that are expanded on in the later narrative report, sometimes called the full report. Top-line reports vary in length but are usually several pages long.

BACKGROUND

Example of an Outline for a Written Report

1. Cover Page. The front cover often includes the title, names of people receiving or commissioning the report, the names of the researchers, and the date the report is submitted.

2. Summary. The brief, well-written executive summary describes why focus groups were conducted and lists major findings and recommendations. The summary is often limited to two pages and should be able to stand alone. Although this section is placed first in the written report, it is often the last part written.

3. Table of Contents. This section isn't needed if the report is short but does help readers navigate longer reports.

4. Purpose and Procedures. Describe the purpose of the study and include a brief description of the study. Remember your audience. Academics may want a detailed description of procedures, but most readers aren't interested in much beyond the number of groups, types of people included as participants, and where the groups were held. The questions are not included here but may be included in the appendix. Sometimes a more detailed discussion of procedures or methods is included in the appendix.

5. Results or Findings. Most often, results are organized around key questions, themes, or big ideas. The conventional style is to take the questions in sequence. The limitation is that this style begins with the least important information (the more valuable results usually occur later in the focus group). Also, information is often redundant because the same themes appear in several questions. Therefore, consider organizing by themes and begin with those points that are most beneficial to the reader.

6. Conclusions/Interpretations. This section is optional. This is the section in which the researchers present their conclusions or interpretations of the results. What do the findings mean? Interpretations can be tricky. If participants in the focus groups provide interpretations, then this information is considered a finding because the participants said it. But if the researcher provides the interpretation, then it belongs in this section. Keep your interpretations separate from the findings.

7. Recommendations. Recommendations are optional and not automatically included in focus group reports. The recommendations provide suggestions as to what might be done with the results. Sometimes this section is presented as "suggestions" or "ideas to consider" or other words that convey less formality.

8. Appendix. The appendix is optional. It includes additional materials that might be helpful to the reader. For example, you might include the questioning route and the screening questionnaire. Additional quotations may also be included. In some situations, the author might wish to include limitations and alternative interpretations.

The top-line report is sometimes confused with the executive summary because they are both short. The executive summary is derived from the narrative report analysis, is prepared at the conclusion of the narrative report, and seeks to highlight critical points. By contrast, the top-line report is prepared quickly without benefit of the careful analysis found in the narrative report, and the emphasis of top-line reports is quickness in reporting.

Top-line reports are standard in market research because sponsors want immediate results. Sponsors often view the groups from behind the one-way mirror and will make decisions based on their own impressions if the analyst doesn't quickly provide a report. In many cases in market research, the study is completed by a seasoned moderator and is very focused (e.g., which ad has greatest appeal?), which makes top-line reports straightforward. They are prepared with minimal time for reflection or analysis, so there is great danger of error for novice researchers. The top-line report exists for a particular function—providing rapid results to concerned clients.

Bulleted Report

The bulleted report is like an outline of the narrative report but with careful choice of phrases and words to clearly convey the concepts. The bulleted report is gaining popularity because of the speed with which it can be prepared and consumed.

Report Letter to Participants

Often participants in focus groups will ask if they can get a copy of the report or find out what happened based on their input. If no results are evident, there is a tendency for the participants to assume that the organization is nonresponsive. For example, in some communities of color and in some organizations, people are reluctant to participate in focus groups because they haven't seen results from past listening. They don't believe their input will make a difference because they haven't seen any evidence that the organization is willing to change.

Usually public and nonprofit organizations freely share focus group findings with participants. As one method of sharing, we encourage the sponsoring organization to write a report letter based on one of the reports described above. This report letter is sent to people who participated in the focus groups. It is one or two pages long and tells participants that "we heard you and this is what we plan to do based on what we heard." Often this report letter is sent as a cover letter for an executive summary or a narrative report. The information in the report letter can cover all audiences in the study or can be adapted for a particular audience, emphasizing items of concern for that particular type of group. For example, one letter might be written for parents, a different one for teachers, and yet a different one for students if these audiences raised different concerns in the study.

An effective strategy is to include four items in the report letter. First, thank participants for sharing their ideas and taking the time to participate. Second, include a very short summary of key findings—perhaps three or four bulleted points or a couple paragraphs. Third, tell what you are doing or what you plan to do to address the key findings. If for some reason you can't do anything about something, explain why. Finally, if it seems appropriate, invite participants to call and share their reactions to the report letter or ask for more information. Include a name and phone number. And again, consider attaching a longer version of the report—typically an executive summary or narrative report.

Oral Reports

For some people, giving an oral report is a terrifying experience. It brings up fears of "dry mouth," hostile audiences, and questions that are impossible to answer. Here are some tips that have helped us prepare for oral reports. Experts tend to use these strategies, and indeed, we've learned them by observing people who are good at giving oral reports.

Allow Time for Questions

Before preparing the oral briefing or presentation, find out how much time is available, where the report will be given, and who the audience will be. Those receiving an oral report usually want to discuss findings, respond to the results, or ask questions. The most successful oral reporters allocate only one third to one half of the time for the presentation, and the remainder is spent in follow-up discussion. Therefore, a fifteen-minute report may include a five-minute presentation and ten minutes for questions, clarifications, and discussion of future action.

Cite the Most Important Things First

The first few minutes in an oral report are critical, and the speaker will need to quickly set the stage for the presentation of findings. Carefully lay out the framework describing why the study is important to the audience. The oral presentation must be focused on the key points, citing the most important finding first and then moving to less important findings. Within these first few moments, the speaker should highlight several key factors. For example, Why was the study needed? What do we know now that we didn't know before? How can these findings be used? It is important to quickly engage the audience, involve them in the report, hook them into the study, and explain clearly why the research effort was important.

Some communications experts have recommended that the most important points be presented at the end of an oral presentation—that lesser points build toward a crescendo. This does not work well in evaluation or research reporting, where people receiving the report often have time restrictions and limited patience and where interruptions regularly occur. In these situations, conciseness is valued. Place the most important findings at the top of the list.

Also, the outline used in the written report does not transfer well to oral reporting. Often researchers make the assumption that a report is a report, whether it is oral or written, and that the sequence of information presented should be consistent in both kinds of reports. Oral reporting is different, and it requires special thought and preparation.

Be Careful of Ho-Hum Syndrome

When planning for the oral report, it is helpful to consider the ho-hum syndrome. Ho-hum is best characterized by the questions going through the minds of the audience: "Do we really need this study?" "Don't we know this already?" "We paid to have somebody study this?" or "Shouldn't this staff member be doing something really important instead of conducting these studies?" To us, the results might seem enormously important with far-reaching implications, but to a busy decision maker, they might sound like hairsplitting and avoidance of real work. Often the best procedure is to address it head-on by saying, "This study is important because . . ." Or tell the audience what the other possible hypotheses were, that we now know the correct course of action, and, as a result, time and resources are saved.

Limit Your Points

Try to limit your report to fewer than seven points. Studies in cognitive psychology suggest that most people can remember only five to seven items in short-term memory. Use short, active phrases to describe points as opposed to complete sentences. These brief phrases are designed to do two things: convey the important concepts and be easily remembered.

Use Visuals and Quotes

Visuals can effectively highlight the points. Key points and quotes tend to be memorable when displayed visually. Use drawings from the groups if you used this type of question. Selected quotations or even brief tape recordings of actual comments can also be very effective in the oral report, but they must be used in moderation. (Also, the audience members shouldn't be able to identify the voices because you promised confidentiality. Therefore, don't do this in a work environment where colleagues could identify one another.) When it comes to visuals, the researcher has an array of options at differing levels of technology. One of the most basic is the briefing chart. These can be made on posterboard or foamboard and used to highlight key points. In addition, these charts can be reproduced in smaller 8½-by-11-inch handouts and shared with the audience. Investigate the possibility of using presentation software on your computer. Professional-quality results can be obtained with minimal skill.

Tell Your Audience What You Want Them to Do

Sometimes the purpose of the oral report is unclear to the audience. We have seen oral reports in which group members just looked at each other for a few awkward moments when the report was done. This uncomfortable silence was then followed by some type of action typical of elected bodies. Someone usually moves that the report be approved or accepted. Then they can move on to really important matters. In these situations, the group was never told why it was receiving the briefing. At the beginning or end of the report, the reporter should indicate what action is recommended or why the report is presented, such as to provide a briefing, form a study committee, continue discussion at a later time, seek funds to implement the findings, approve a new course of action, and so on. It is dangerous to assume that the audience will know what to do with the report.

Select the Right Reporter

Some people have a natural or acquired talent for preparing written reports. Others are great at presenting oral reports. Select your reporter based on ability and credibility and not because of his or her role in the focus group study. Some individuals are gifted in presenting findings. Consider these people. As important, however, is the credibility of the reporter. At times, a volunteer or someone from outside of the agency or organization is more credible. ("Of course the project director is going to say they need more money for special education. That's her job!") The best choice is to have an individual who is both skillful and credible present the results.

Naturally, the reporter will need to be sufficiently acquainted with both the process and findings. The reporter should practice the oral report and allow sufficient time for preparation and collegial feedback. Hastily prepared reports often have awkward construction, vague points, misspellings, and other aspects that limit their acceptance by users.

Electronic Reporting

Electronic reporting is a fast-moving trend that will affect all fields of research. New resources, equipment, and software are being developed so fast that it is hard to keep track of changes. The Internet, high capacity storage devices, voice recognition software, and digital recording equipment are having a profound impact on how information is presented and received.

With the Internet, sizable amounts of information can be transmitted virtually instantaneously around the world. Web sites can be set up that allow designated users to view and print reports.

High capacity disks and writable CDs now allow the researcher to include pictures, video, sound, and text together in a low-cost format. New recording equipment allows the researcher to capture video or audio materials in a digital format. Quality is superior to that of analog recorders, and with new software, the researcher can easily locate, edit, and present results of focus group interviews.

Here are some possibilities:

- A report could include:
  Digital photographs of people, products, places, and so on
  Video clips of participants commenting on the topic
  Audio clips of participants
  Attractively formatted text
  (Confidentiality may be an issue with some of these options)
- The report could be saved on a writable CD disk and made available to designated individuals.
- The report could be placed on a Web site and made available to any person with access information.
- The report could be presented at a small or large group meeting using a laptop computer along with a projector or large-screen display.

Be careful! Don't use these techniques just because they are possible. If your audience doesn't use computers, then CD disks and Web sites don't make sense. As you ponder the decision about if and when to use technology, also consider the resources needed in terms of talent, hardware, software, and staff time. One of the constant dangers of reporting is that the technology—the gimmicks—can get in the way of the message. The viewer is so distracted by the visual effect that the message is overlooked. Technology is seductive. Don't let your message get lost in the silicon jungle.

SUMMARY

Many judge the quality of a focus group study by the report. Take the time and effort needed to produce top quality reporting. We offer five principles of reporting that have helped us and have served as a valuable checklist during the reporting phase of the study. The focus group researcher will need to make a decision about which types of reporting to use: written, oral, or electronic. Use a combination of approaches whenever possible.

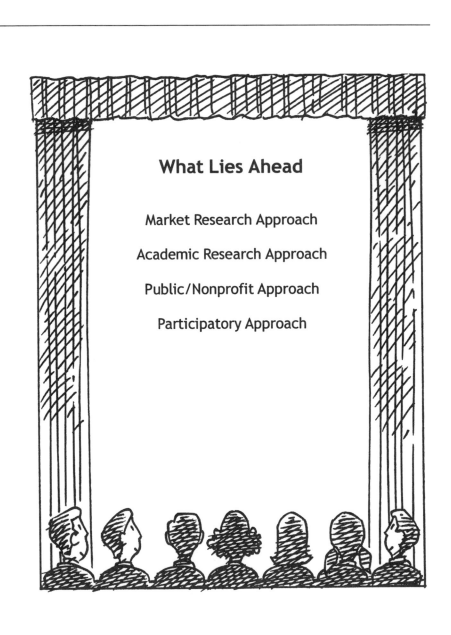

8

Styles of Focus Group Research

O ver the past sixty years, focus group research has evolved so that we now have several approaches—market research, academic, public/nonprofit, and participatory. Knowing these approaches can be helpful when reviewing focus group literature, contracting for focus group research, or just learning about alternative procedures. If you don't know these various approaches exist, you may be confused by differences you see in focus groups. Let's compare these approaches.

Market Research Approach

Market research focus groups have been used and refined over the past half-century. It was the market researchers who sought practicality, usefulness, fast turnaround, and economic benefit. They weren't bound intellectually to academics' concerns about contamination and analysis and instead were driven by straightforward economic concerns. Does the information help us produce a better product? Can our business profit from the information obtained?

Let's look at some of the traditions in for-profit market research focus groups.

Market researchers have built the focus group interview into an industry with special focus group facilities, rooms with one-way mirrors, special procedures for recruiting participants, guidelines on the size of focus groups, cash incentives, and professional moderators.

Special focus group rooms with one-way mirrors became standard operating procedure for these commercial, market research focus groups. For a time, some companies had their own rooms, but these weren't helpful when they wanted to listen to consumers in another part of the country. Soon, special focus group facilities appeared in major cities around the country. Typically, these facilities offer several rooms with one-way mirrors and audio- and videotaping options, professional screening and recruiting services to locate focus group participants, meeting rooms for clients to use, and catering services for the clients and participants.

The viewing rooms allow the sponsors of the research and others (advertising team, marketing staff, engineers, product developers, etc.) to observe consumers talking about the product. This firsthand observation is highly instructive for executives, who are often unfamiliar with the day-by-day realities of ordinary consumers. Watching the groups allows the sponsor to see the product through the eyes of the customer. Moreover, it provides new ideas for creative designers as they develop new products and services.

Most market research groups were and still are conducted with white, middle-class, suburban and urban residents because typically, the goal is to learn how to sell more of a product or service. As a result, the focus groups were conducted with people who had disposable income. In recent years, marketers have begun seeking out greater diversity in race and age, provided, of course, that they are a target market for the product or service.

Recruiting participants is big business for these facilities. Recruiters phone people, screen them, and invite them to the groups. Participants are offered money as an incentive to show up. The harder the type of person is to find, the more they are paid to show up. Some market researchers are very concerned about how often people participate in focus groups. Some participants enjoy the opportunity to talk, listen to others, and get paid and make an effort to get into groups. They have been labeled *focus groupies*. Market researchers fear that repeat participants will alter the results of focus group research. So nationwide screening services have been developed to discover if a particular potential participant has been in a focus group in the past few months. This concern is unique to commercial market research focus groups.

Group size was set at ten to twelve participants. This appears to be based on the field experiences of moderators. It may have been that moderators found that a portion of participants were often reluctant to talk, sometimes as many as 30%, and if you invited a dozen people, you would almost always have enough "talkers" to provide information. In addition, moderators found that groups of more than twelve were harder to manage, tended to fragment into smaller conversations, and did not yield proportionally more insights. Some researchers even recruit fifteen people and select ten to twelve to participate. The others are given the incentive for showing up and sent on their way.

Businesses hire professional focus group moderators to conduct their studies. There is a network of these people throughout the country. People learn to be market research moderators by taking classes and by being an apprentice to a master moderator. Some firms have aspiring moderators observe and assist for several years before they moderate a group. They receive practical experience and coaching. (This is the only time assistant researchers are used in commercial focus groups because it is an added expense. They sit behind the one-way mirror, take notes, and may be responsible for writing a first draft of a report.)

Speedy results are essential in market research groups. Professional market researcher moderators complain that clients want final reports within days of the last focus group. They do not have time to do elaborate analysis based on transcripts. Reports are considered proprietary information and are rarely available to the public.

BACKGROUND

If you would like to read more about focus groups using a market research approach, you might consider the following:

Goldman, A. E., & McDonald, S. S. (1987). *The group depth interview.* Englewood Cliffs, NJ: Prentice Hall.

Greenbaum, T. L. (1998). *The handbook for focus group research.* Thousand Oaks, CA: Sage.

Academic Research Approach

Even though academics created the focused interview, the academic community did not embrace the method at first. For some time, academics were apprehensive about focus group interviews because of the difficulties in analysis and the seeming contamination of the interview process. Academics were concerned because in focus group interviews, people talked to one another. They heard each other's views. Also, individual respondents sometimes expressed different and even opposite opinions. Participants were not always consistent! This phenomenon had not been seen in individual interviews, and it was now a concern when it occurred in group discussions. Were people

influencing each other? Was this an example of contamination? Were some people with strong personalities dominating others? The group process seemed uncontrolled, confusing, and complex. Academics weren't able to neatly isolate influencing factors.

But the success of focus groups in the market research environment did not go unnoticed. Academics began to reexamine the potential for focus group research in the early 1980s. Some were wondering if focus groups could get a different kind of information than individual interviews or surveys. They could. For example, in our work on needs assessments with Midwest farmers, we found that the survey process wasn't providing useable results. Later we discovered in focus groups that we weren't asking the "right" questions. We thought farmers would attend educational sessions if they indicated they needed the information on a needs assessment survey. But farmers told us in focus groups, "Just because I need it, doesn't mean I'll go." The right question became, "What would it take to get you to go?" They said they were more likely to go if:

- the experience seemed like it would be fun,
- there was an opportunity to meet other farmers,
- the course seemed useful and was being taught by someone who had practical experience ("grease under their fingernails"), and
- if they were personally told it would be a good course by someone they trusted, such as their veterinarian or banker or another farmer.

All of these findings made sense, and we wondered why we hadn't thought of them earlier. We had trapped ourselves into thinking that attendance was primarily influenced by a perception of need for the subject.

When academic researchers began doing focus groups, they built on their rich experiences with individual interviewing and content analysis. The academics brought with them several strategies and traditions that were distinctly different from the contributions of market researchers.

Openness was foremost. Although in the past, the proprietary reports of market researchers were confidential and access was severely restricted for fear of helping the competition, this type of confidentiality was not in the tradition of academics. In fact, their tradition was quite the opposite. The position of the academic was, "Unless my colleagues know how I recruited participants, conducted the groups, and performed the analysis, how can they adequately critique my work?" Openness was essential to academic adoption. Academic promotion was influenced by peer review and publication in refereed journals, and these factors demanded that colleagues be able to see the details of the process.

Rigor was expected. The analysis process no longer was secret. It wasn't done in closed environments with restricted access. Now the results were available, and other researchers were invited to look over the analysis protocol and comment. Analysis had to be defensible, systematic, and verifiable. Some of the earlier market research analysis was done mentally, in the heads of moderators based on memory and a few notes. This was not acceptable in an academic environment. The data had to be captured in multiple forms—field notes and audiotapes. Transcripts were used in the analysis. Researchers used computer software analysis programs as they coded, categorized, and interpreted the findings.

Timing took on a different meaning. Academics were under a very different timeframe than were the market researchers. Quality academic research took time—often months or years to complete. By contrast, market researchers needed to have results ready in hours or days.

People in academic environments learn to do focus groups by reading, taking courses, and doing the research. Unless a graduate student is lucky, there is not much coaching because faculty members are juggling a dozen different things, and there isn't time for individual mentoring. Graduate students often help or even conduct a fair amount of the research. At times, the goal of academic research is not just to provide defensible results but also to enhance the capacity of these graduate students. Sometimes faculty add elements to the design because it enriches the learning opportunities of the graduate student. For example, sometimes graduate students are asked to transcribe their focus groups. Not a popular thing to ask of a graduate student! Probably a professional typist could type it faster, but then the graduate student would not have the intense familiarity needed to undertake later analysis steps.

The location of the research changed. Academics went to the target audience. The special focus group rooms were often in the wrong locations, too intimidating, or too expensive. As a result, academics began using alternative locations such as homes, public meeting rooms, and restaurants.

The audience changed. Academics, in general, were less concerned about consumer products. Their attention was on issues such as public health, education, the environment, and policy issues. As a result, many different types of people were invited to focus groups. This included low-income audiences, people of color, people who had difficulty speaking English, youth, international audiences, and others.

Academics also started to provide incentives for participation. Although monetary incentives had been used to encourage people to participate in medical research, it was less common in other fields. Researchers needed to develop processes for providing these incentives.

BACKGROUND

If you would like to read more about focus groups using an academic research approach, you might consider the following:

Morgan, D. L. (1997). *Focus groups as qualitative research.* Thousand Oaks, CA: Sage.
Vaughn, S., Schummn, J. S., & Sinagub, J. (1996). *Focus group interviews in education and psychology.* Thousand Oaks, CA: Sage.

Public/Nonprofit Approach

At about the same time that academics were beginning to use focus groups, another group became interested in the focus group methodology. The public/nonprofit approach began to emerge. In the academic approach, the intent was to develop theory or to contribute to a body of research in a particular area. In the public/nonprofit approach, the purpose was usually more immediate and practical.

Some were concerned about how well they were doing, how to improve, how to attract more members, or how to keep members. Some wanted to know how to improve their community. Some wanted to know how to design a policy or program so people would use it. The studies were sometimes called needs assessments, formative evaluations, process evaluations, climate studies, or customer satisfaction studies. The purpose was not to develop theory but rather to make decisions, improve services or programs, and be responsive to customers. These groups had some similarity to the market research focus groups, except the product had changed.

Religious groups began to ask about what their members wanted. Interesting questions emerged, such as, "What is worship?" "How can a religious group add meaning to your life?" "How can the church help you?" "What would it take to get you to participate in religious activities?" In some ways, this was a switch because many of these religious organizations historically told participants the answers to such questions instead of listening to their members.

Public health professionals were among the first to embrace focus group interviewing. Those working in prevention campaigns or in the emerging field of social marketing were quick to see the potential of focus groups. They borrowed many strategies from consumer marketing and adapted them to new products, services, and audiences. It was these public health professionals who were most aggressive in reaching new audiences. Academics had made some inroads, but it was the public health professionals who went into the neighborhoods, schools, WIC clinics, and migrant worker camps and listened. The driving force was need. Low-income, disadvantaged, young, and other marginalized populations were included when new programs were designed. Public health professionals now listen widely when they design programs to increase breast-feeding or vaccinations or to prevent tobacco use, teen pregnancy, and violence.

Educational and service organizations began to use focus groups to determine what customers or potential customers wanted. How do adults want to learn? What topics are important? How should the agency deliver its services or products?

Government agencies began to use focus groups. Sometimes the studies related to employee satisfaction, such as when the postal service was concerned about employee morale. Other times, a unit of government wanted insight into customer satisfaction. In other situations, focus groups were helpful in developing policies, rules, guidelines, and laws that were understandable and reasonable to the public. There is nothing more expensive to enforce than an unreasonable or ambiguous law. Focus groups provided ideas about what would work.

Some organizations were interested in designing new programs or services and wanted to understand how potential participants saw the issue. Or they wanted to pilot test ideas for programs. "What do you like about this idea?" "What don't you like?" "What will it take to make this work?"

These public/nonprofit groups are different from market research and academic focus groups in several ways.

These groups are smaller than traditional market research focus groups. Instead of ten to twelve participants, the groups tend to have six to eight participants. Smaller groups allow each person a greater opportunity to talk. It allows for more in-depth conversation. Also, living rooms and dining room tables are more suitable for six to eight people as opposed to a dozen people.

The moderator changed. Instead of a professional moderator or an academic, the moderator is often an internal person with skills in evaluation, group process, or interviewing. Sometimes it is a volunteer from the community who is trusted and respected by the participants. Regularly, in these groups, the most critical moderator skill is to develop a trusting environment. On sensitive topics—how I feel about merit pay, morale within the organization, or how I deal with a health problem—participants are often more comfortable with a moderator who seems like them or is someone they trust.

The locations were typically within the community. One-way mirrors don't work with these topics. These focus groups were not a spectator sport. They were trusting, confidential sharing experiences in a small group.

The time spent on analysis ranges from the quick market research approach to the academic approach, depending on the audience and purpose of the groups. Often these groups want to know what the five to seven most important things are to pay attention to. This usually doesn't require detailed analysis using specialized computer software. But because those using the information to make decisions often don't get a chance to see the groups (no one-way mirror), they do want a report that provides enough evidence to make the findings credible.

These groups are usually quite open. Researchers let the participants and the community know the results of the study and the subsequent action steps. Care is taken to ensure confidentiality of each participant, but findings are freely shared.

BACKGROUND

If you would like to read more about focus groups using a public/ nonprofit approach, you might consider the following:

Debus, M. (1990). *Handbook for excellence in focus group research.* Washington, DC: Academy for Educational Development.

Morgan, D. L., & Krueger, R. A. (Eds.). (1998). *The focus group kit.* Thousand Oaks, CA: Sage.

Participatory Approach

By the early 1990s, another approach to focus group research was emerging—that of getting nonresearchers involved in the process. Up to this point, the prevailing wisdom was that only researchers could do research. Research had to be done in a particular way, and it required training and experience to do it well.

The evolution is a bit fuzzy, but many of the early participatory approaches were driven by lack of resources, particularly when monies were tight. Information was needed, budgets were restricted, and some creative researchers began to enlist the help of volunteers. These volunteers offered their time and talent and thereby saved precious resources. They obtained useful data, and the process offered some unexpected benefits. The volunteers were changed! The process often influenced the volunteers in ways that were not anticipated. The volunteers now had greater insight into the program or topic. They became committed to the study and were tenacious in seeing that recommendations were followed. To many researchers, this was a surprising discovery. For years, evaluators and other researchers were concerned about how to get people to use research and evaluation results, and now one answer seemed to emerge. If you want them to use it, then involve them in the process. The involvement couldn't be just tokenism but had to be a real, sincere sharing of power in the research study. The volunteers were not just workers but were partners and co-researchers. Often this meant training, considerable coaching, lots of coordination, and learning to give up some control.

The participatory approach does have limitations. Consistency and coordination are major issues. The team members sometimes change a few questions or leave out some questions. Questions are sometimes asked differently from one group to another. Keeping the team working together is a major challenge. Training is critically important, especially hands-on experiences in which volunteers get to practice their skills. Decision making sometimes becomes an issue. How does the researcher work within a community that wants and demands a shared role in decision making—including decisions about the research design and protocol? For some researchers, it is frustrating and stressful. Others relish the opportunity.

BACKGROUND

If you would like to read more about focus groups using a participatory approach, you might consider the following:

Krueger, R. A., & King, J. A. (1998). *Involving community members in focus groups.* Thousand Oaks, CA: Sage.

Table 8.1 offers some highlights of the distinctions between these four focus group approaches.

TABLE 8.1 Characteristics of Focus Groups

Characteristic	Market Research	Academic	Nonprofit and Public	Participatory
Where popular?	Commercial businesses	Universities, government agencies, foundations	Governments, community groups, foundations	Community groups, schools, foundations, local government
Group size?	Ten to twelve people	Six to eight people	Six to eight people	Six to eight people
Should participants know each other?	No. Strangers preferred	Not an issue. People may know each other but are not in positions of control over each other.	Not an issue. Sometimes it is an advantage, provided they are not in positions of control over each other.	Sometimes an advantage. People regularly know each other.
Who moderates?	Professionals	Faculty, graduate students, or qualified staff	Qualified staff and occasional volunteers with special skills	Volunteers from the community
Where are focus groups held?	Special rooms with one-way mirrors and quality acoustics	Public locations, classrooms, sometimes homes, or special rooms with one-way mirrors	Locations in the community, such as schools, libraries, and so on	Community locations and homes

(continued)

TABLE 8.1 Continued

Characteristic	Market Research	Academic	Nonprofit and Public	Participatory
How are data captured?	Observers behind mirrors, audio and often video recording	Field notes and audio recording. Sometimes video.	Field notes and audio recording	Field notes and audio recording
How are results analyzed?	Variable but often rapid first impressions given by moderator or analyst. Sometimes transcripts.	Usually transcripts followed by rigorous procedures	Usually abridged transcripts and field notes	Oral summaries at conclusion, flip charts, field notes, listening to audiotapes
Who gets copies of reports?	Only the sponsor. Reports are proprietary.	Academics or public officials. Results appear in academic journals.	Reports used within the organization and sent back to the community. Shared with participants.	Considerable effort made to share results with the community.
Time needed to complete study?	Short time period. Usually completed in a few weeks.	Long time period. Often six months or more.	Time needed will vary. Usually takes several months.	Long time period. Often six months or more.

SUMMARY

We have observed four different styles to focus group research. The market research approach is by far the most popular and widely recognized. In fact, market research focus groups have become a well-established, extensive industry with professional moderators, special focus group facilities, and an assortment of added services to assist in recruitment, screening, recording, transcribing, and analyzing results. When people talk of focus groups, it is the market research focus group that typically comes to mind. These groups are distinguished by their tendency to include 10 to 12 participants gathered in a special room equipped with a one-way mirror.

But other styles are emerging and are making distinct contributions to our understanding of focus group research. The academic research approach incorporates openness, rigor, and peer review. The public/nonprofit approach borrows elements from the academic research tradition in terms of careful analysis and openness but then seeks to be more decision oriented as opposed to developing theory. Finally, the participatory approach is drawing interest mostly because of what it does to develop commitment and interest.

We offer these categories as a way of letting people know that not all focus group studies use the same approach. Of course, these four categories aren't mutually exclusive. We have been involved in studies where academics are working with a public agency. Team members want to publish in academic journals and make practical decisions based on the study. And public agencies often engage community groups in participatory focus groups.

In the coming decades, other styles will emerge that will reflect other needs. Throughout all these styles, the focus groups still retain their distinctive quality of having a planned discussion using predetermined questions, guided by a skillful moderator, conducted in a permissive and nonthreatening manner, for the purposes of providing insight.

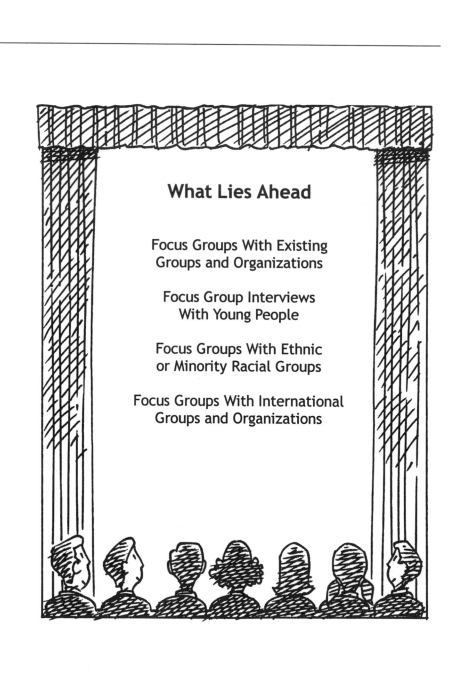

Adapting Focus Groups to Audiences and Environments

Much of what we know about focus groups is based on white, middle-class, adult American consumers. But this research procedure works regardless of level of race, socioeconomic class, age, or education, as long as the researcher is respectful of the limitations of focus groups. International researchers have taken focus groups to Costa Rica, Morocco, Thailand, India, and a host of other countries with positive experiences. Others have successfully conducted focus groups with migrant workers, inner-city residents, teenagers, people who suffer from psychoses, people with developmental disabilities, and American Indians—people who often don't get asked for their input or get listened to.

Throughout all of these groups, there is a hidden challenge. Unwittingly, the focus group researcher may ask irrelevant questions—those that reflect the researcher's experiences and point of view but seem inappropriate, irrelevant, or impractical to the participants. This phenomenon is more likely to occur in the public and nonprofit sectors where cross-cultural studies are conducted.

One area where we have observed variation is in how people differ in their sense of control. Some individuals feel they have control over their environment and that other individuals can and ought to make needed changes. Others feel that someone has control, but they personally do not. Still others feel that no one has control or that one should not tamper with fate but rather accept what comes your way. If you are examining a public program or the consequence of a policy decision, each group might offer a different perspective based on its philosophical orientation. In fact, we would argue that the participants might not even understand the question because it is so different from their worldview. Questions need to be constructed carefully and the study introduced in a manner appropriate to the environment.

Four types of special audiences deserve attention. One category is internal focus groups. A second category is focus groups with young people. A third special audience is focus groups within ethnically or racially homogeneous audiences. And the fourth category consists of groups sponsored by international organizations.

Focus Groups With Existing Groups and Organizations

Although the focus group process is robust, there are several situations in which additional caution is needed. One area requiring caution is in using focus groups with existing groups, especially workers within an organization. In these environments, participants not only know each other but are often familiar with the values, habits, and interests of their colleagues. Focus groups with these existing work groups present several challenges. The first challenge is to create an environment where employees are willing to openly share their concerns, anxieties, and suggestions. The organizational climate may restrict open communication and discourage or even punish alternative points of view. Also, although knowing one another may promote sharing with one group, it may inhibit sharing in another group.

Despite these difficulties, focus groups can be used effectively in existing organizations and even in work groups.

TIP

Focus Groups With Existing Groups and Organizations

1. Control the sampling strategy.
2. Use care when placing participants in groups.
3. Be aware of environment and recent history.
4. Select the right moderator.
5. Provide adequate confidentiality.
6. Provide benefit to participants.
7. Do a reality check after each group.
8. Analyze with group dynamics in mind.

Perhaps the foremost problem facing the researcher is the manner in which participants are selected. Convenience samples—that is, selecting people because they are easy to recruit—are dangerous with internal groups. In the same vein, another dangerous practice is relying on insiders to select people by memory, past experiences, or other criteria. Memories are faulty, and bias can easily creep into the selection. The researcher should develop a sampling plan specifying the screens or criteria for participation in the focus group and follow it carefully. We suggest using the old standby process of developing a "pool" of people who meet screening requirements and then randomly selecting from this pool. Often the researcher is unfamiliar with the organization and must rely on insiders to provide advice on sample selection. In some situations, this insider insight can be of great benefit, but in other situations, there are inadvertent biases.

Care should be exercised when placing participants into groups. In general, avoid power differentials. This can vary by organization and tradition, but the participants should feel that they are in a group with people of equivalent position. Avoid situations in which supervisors and subordinates are in the same focus group. In addition, the researcher should be aware that preestablished small groups are more difficult to analyze. For these groups, communication is exceedingly complex. Instead, if possible, place people with other colleagues. This forces participants to explain their comments more fully and completely and to rely less on the cryptic communication.

Learn the organizational environment and recent history. Outside researchers are often unfamiliar with the culture, traditions, and communication styles within organizations. To what extent is this an organization where people openly share ideas? Do they value the insight of others, and are they respectful of divergent views? Interestingly, sometimes even internal staff may not be aware of these messages (regarding respect, tolerance, valuing opinions of others, listening, openness to new ideas, etc.) that are informally communicated within the organization. Here are some views that we've found within organizations that limit focus group usage.

"If you see the problem and say something about it, then you are expected to find the solution. Therefore, don't mention the problem."

"Management says they want advice, but they've already made the decision."

"It's OK to be critical, but only with certain other insiders. Certain topics are so sacred that they are talked about with only the closest of friends."

Perhaps the most effective way to become grounded in the organizational climate is to conduct individual, informal interviews with a variety of staff as the study is being designed. By chatting with employees, the researcher can get advice about a number of logistical aspects of the study, test potential questions, and generally discover what is needed to make the study a success.

It regularly takes extra effort to create a nonthreatening, permissive environment in internal groups. Employees need to feel comfortable with the study. We go to extra lengths to let people know "who asked for the information," "what prompted the study," "what kind of decisions are going to be made based on the information," and "who is going to listen to the tapes." Avoid creating the impression that the organization will do what one group suggests. Participants are reminded that information is being gathered from a number of groups of employees, and then these aggregated perceptions will be shared with those who will be making decisions.

Know the limits of focus group research. In these organizational environments, it may be impossible to create the necessary focus group conditions. Know when to avoid focus group research. If participants don't trust the sponsor or their colleagues, see the study as a threat, or are unwilling to listen to views of others, then focus groups are unlikely to work.

Who should moderate? Moderators from outside the organization have the advantage of being neutral, but they may be unfamiliar with the organizational culture. External moderators may see things internal moderators wouldn't because they have a chance to compare this environment with others. Internal moderators are more familiar with the organization but need to be viewed as someone who can listen, who can be trusted, and that it makes sense they would be asking about the topic. For example, it would make sense for someone from the human resources department to be asking about morale or benefits. When selecting a moderator, weigh the advantages and disadvantages of internal and external moderators.

Confidentiality is a sensitive issue with internal focus groups. Once again, the concern over confidentiality will likely be triggered by the topic, the organizational culture, and traditions. Does the organization welcome divergent and different ideas? In the past, what has happened to people who have been critical? No promise from the moderator will be trusted if past promises haven't been held. The moderator should be clear and open about the nature of the promise. It often begins at the planning stage with decision makers who are requesting the study. Be absolutely clear about who has access to participant names. This usually means that those requesting the study will not have access to participant lists.

Confidentiality also needs to be respected by others in the focus group. The moderator must be clear about what behaviors are expected in the group. It defeats the purpose when the moderator promises confidentiality but then a focus group participant later tells everyone they know what others have said in the group. Consider including these things in your introduction to the focus group:

- Describe the study. Include who asked for it and why.
- Tell who has access to the results.
- Describe how results will benefit participants or the organization.
- Give a general promise of confidentiality by the researchers, which means no names are attached.
- Tell how audiotapes will be used. Who will have access to them?
- Request that the group also maintain confidentiality for each other.
- Explain that the moderator's role is to guide the discussion and keep it on track. On some topics, the moderator may ask to talk to you individually after the group.
- Explain that no names are wanted—so please don't mention names of colleagues.
- Tell them the moderator will summarize key points of the discussion at the end and then ask for help to ensure that we've captured the most important points.

Be able to describe the benefit of the study. In particular, describe how the participants and their colleagues will benefit directly or indirectly. In many cases, the benefit is for colleagues, neighbors, and friends. "What is learned from the study will improve services to other veterans," "This study will help top management make decisions about merit pay and employee benefits," or "This study will help us better serve our patients." The promise must be reasonable and sufficiently specific to be credible. Keep in mind that at the end of the study the researchers should deliver on this promise by describing the results and showing how they are linked to the goals.

Do a reality check after each group. At the end of the focus group, add a few questions about the study. In our experience, we've found it helpful to ask the ending questions, provide a brief summary, and ask for verification and then turn off the tape recorder. But don't excuse the participants just yet. Tell them that you are finished with the more formal part of the discussion, and now you would like their advice on the process. Indicate that this is just to help the research team improve later discussions. Then, ask a few questions about the process. It could be as simple as, "Well, what did you think of the discussion?" or "What can I do to improve the discussion?" or "What can I do to make people more comfortable?" If you suspect they may have held back, you might ask, "Do you think people will hold back and not tell us what they are really thinking?"

When doing the analysis, keep in mind that certain discussion patterns are common to existing groups. Veteran analysts have noticed that when all participants are members of the group, there is a tendency to be overly harsh on the sponsoring organization or institution. If there is a mix of insiders and outsiders, participants may be more restrained in their criticism. In addition, insiders know more about how the organization works, what has been promised, and what promises haven't been met. All of this can fuel cynicism, provoke anger, and make participants skeptical of the study's intent. Participants may have another agenda that they wish to follow in the focus groups, such as persuasion, blocking, or promotion. Because participants know each other and have developed relationships with other participants, the discussion can be affected in a variety of ways. In effect, the focus group participants are reacting to both the ideas expressed and the people expressing those ideas. It may be difficult or impossible to determine if the reaction is to the other person or the idea. Be watchful and alert.

Focus Group Interviews With Young People

Focus groups have considerable potential for discovering how young people think about issues, programs, and opportunities, but focus groups with young people are different from those of adults. For example, young people lack control over their environment. They are

TIP

Focus Groups With Young People

1. Get the right moderator.
2. Keep age range within two years.
3. Get them talking to each other.
4. Ask age-appropriate questions.
5. Be aware of age-related behaviors.
6. Shorten the length of the group.
7. Use food.
8. Find a friendly location.
9. Get permission.
10. Hang loose.

usually in situations where adults have control, and sometimes the rules for behavior are unclear. As a result, young people may be skeptical of the moderator's claim that all opinions are wanted and that both negative and positive views are appreciated. Young people regularly find themselves in situations where adults seemingly want feedback but then react in an unpleasant manner when contrary or negative ideas are expressed. Furthermore, youth peer pressure is powerful and can greatly shape opinions.

Keep in mind that when asked for their opinions, young people will have fewer life experiences to draw on than adults. "I don't know" can sometimes be the truly accurate answer. When listening to kids, one regularly hears phrases and concepts that really sound like they came from parents, teachers, or religious groups, or are a reflection of societal values. Here are some tips that will make these groups more successful.

Get the right moderator! Some adults really like being around kids. These adults have special talents. They have a knack for getting kids to talk, probably because they exude trust, respect, tolerance, humor, and a willingness to listen. They know how to talk to kids, how to listen to them, how to joke and have fun with them. A number of teachers, youth workers, and volunteers in Scouts, 4H, and so on have these skills. These adults are easy to spot because kids will be around them, there will often be laughter, and they will be talking to each other. If you have to conduct focus groups with young people and you've not been around them recently, find one of these adults and get his or her help.

Another alternative is to have an older teen conduct the group. Maybe a high school or college-age person moderates the group of younger people. Provide the teen moderators with special instruction and considerable practice before they conduct the focus groups. In our experience, the decision on youth versus adult moderators is a toss-up. In several recent prevention efforts, focus groups of youth in Grades seven through eleven were conducted by high school age moderators. The results were impressive and convinced the sponsoring organization of the wisdom of involving youth moderators. The teen-led groups were successful in part because they had removed the image of adult authority, and that prompted sharing on sensitive topics. The decisive factor in conducting successful focus groups, however, is less likely to be the moderator's age and more likely to relate to their ability to get young people to feel comfortable with the topic, the process, and the environment.

Be attentive to the age range of participants. The generally accepted rule is to have an age range of no more than two years among participants. Developmentally, youth change a great deal over a period of two years, and their interests, experiences, and socialization can be dramatically different. Also, youth can be very age conscious and have been known to dismiss valuable comments merely because a younger person said them. Or younger participants may defer to older participants.

Skillful moderators of youth focus groups make extra efforts to get the young people talking to each other at the beginning of the group. Adults know that they are expected to listen and talk to each other, but don't assume that youth will be aware of this expectation. Youth are exposed to so many different game rules that they regularly are uncertain how adults expect them to act. Should they talk to each other? Or is that frowned on? Do you have to raise your hand? In a number of situations, you get punished if you talk to other kids. So, the moderator must not only say that they can talk to each other but also model the behavior and encourage the kids to share ideas. Use questions that get kids talking to each other—and not the moderator—early in the discussion. Ask the young people to be respectful of other opinions and listen to what others have to say, but then share their points of view.

Young people are able to communicate in many ways such as through art, drama, pictures, music, and fantasies. Questions that ask young people to act out the answers, tell stories, or create something can be powerful.

Questions are also different in that there are fewer questions. Instead of the standard ten to twelve questions, you might have six to eight questions. As much as ten or fifteen minutes at the beginning of the group might be dedicated to getting acquainted with other teens. The nature of focus group questions may need some special thought when working with young people. Avoid dichotomous questions that can be answered with a yes or no. Adults may assume that the moderator really wants elaboration on the answer, but young people often give one-word answers. Avoid questions that threaten the independence and freedom of young people. For example, suppose the moderator wanted to know how decisions were made about which high school courses to enroll in. In this situation, the moderator should avoid asking who makes the decision, for few teens want to admit in front of their peers that their parents influence the decision. Instead, it may be more productive to ask teens to think back to the last time the decision was made and describe what happened.

Veteran moderators of youth focus groups tell of specific age-related behaviors. Focus groups of kids younger than age nine are difficult because kids of this age haven't had many group experiences in which they are expected to listen to others before they respond. Focus groups at junior high age (ages twelve to fourteen) are chaotic, and it's wise to keep boys and girls separate, even on mundane topics. After age fourteen or fifteen, youth seem to be better at listening and sharing views and slightly less affected by gender differences than those of junior high age. However, some moderators always separate kids by gender because boys tend to be more active.

Elementary age boys goof off a lot. Get yourself ready. You won't believe what they do unless you've got one of your own. Boys will put the name tents on their heads, fall off their chairs, compete in performance nose blowing, and play with anything on the table. They wave their hands wildly while someone else is talking, only to say, "Uh, I forgot" when called on. They seem to want the attention of others. When you've got eight little guys who want attention at the same time, you're gonna have fun.

Elementary age girls generally won't engage in such behavior. They seem to be better at listening to one another and participating in a discussion.

One age-related behavior is that of forming tight-knit groups. When conducting youth focus groups, researchers tend to prefer groups that are not preestablished. Cohesive groups and cliques may provide a narrow range of views that are heavily influenced by peer leaders. As a result, researchers often prefer to assemble groups of relative strangers.

We usually limit focus groups with young people to sixty minutes or less, especially with preteen audiences. Young people repeatedly find themselves in environments where change or relocation takes place every forty-five to sixty minutes. If the researcher has a two-hour focus group discussion, it is likely that there will be a bunch of bored kids for the second hour. Therefore, limit the questions and, if possible, incorporate things to touch, do, or respond to.

Food is magic. Pizza, snacks, and soda make the discussion more comfortable, relaxed, and enjoyable. Talk to the young people before you select the food. Get their advice on what to serve.

Be cautious about the location. Some locations, such as schools, represent places where young people are subordinate to adults. Homes of other youth, restaurants, and public meeting places are usually considered more neutral. In many studies, the location may not be important, but in certain places, adults are clearly in authority and may have rules about the topic, such as smoking. Then it is best to leave the adult-controlled environment and use a neutral location.

Typically, you need parental permission when conducting youth focus groups. The researcher should contact the sponsoring and cooperating organizations to determine proper protocol regarding parent or guardian approval. In some cases, when the focus group is part of ongoing organizational activity—such as in fitting within objectives of the school and also conducted during school hours—then permission may not be essential. The need for permission for youth focus groups has a double purpose. The first purpose is to meet legal expectations of informing the child and parent. The second purpose is to adequately inform the parent of the proposed focus group interview. In a number of cases, researchers have wisely gone above and beyond the letter of the law and provided considerable background information to parents or guardians.

Finally, be ready to hang loose. Youth focus groups are fun, in part because the unexpected happens regularly. The variation from group to group is greater than with adult groups, and there is excitement around every corner. Keep your sense of humor, show respect, and be ready to improvise.

Focus Groups With Ethnic or Minority Racial Groups

Focus groups are increasingly being used to assess needs or test program materials for ethnic or minority racial groups. In fact, this is one of the growth areas in market research focus groups. This is occurring because there are increasing numbers of people in these target markets, and these people have greater disposable income than in the past. In addition, a number of nonprofit and public agencies are using focus groups with low-income groups and with communities of color. These groups require some special consideration in planning and conducting. Let's review some of the factors.

When planning these racial-ethnic groups, the researcher should keep in mind that there are many ways in which people of one ethnic or racial category are alike and different. Too often, we assume that the homogeneity should be primarily by race. Caution is needed because if race or ethnicity is assumed by the researcher to be the dominant or only distinguishing factor, then you may overlook other critical factors such as income, education, age, gender, culture, or language. If race is used as the dominant factor of homogeneity, then there is a tendency for race to become the major issue.

A strategy to consider is to use several different groupings of participants. Some groups might consist of one racial/ethnic category, but then others might be based on geography, income, age, or other factors. This allows the researcher the opportunity to compare and contrast the results.

TIP

Focus Groups With Ethnic or Minority Racial Groups

1. Sample carefully.
2. Get the right moderator.
3. Stay in touch with locals.
4. Be aware of recent events and history.
5. Ritual can be important.
6. Select respectful and appropriate foods.
7. Ask people to speak for themselves.

Usually one of the first areas of concern is who should moderate these groups. There are often advantages in having a moderator with characteristics similar to the participants. Many of these groups have historically been controlled and guided by white people in positions of power and influence. As a result, there may be a tendency to assume that other individuals from the outside, particularly those who are white, possess power and want information to maintain that influence. Within some groups, there is a tendency to be cautious about talking to outsiders, particularly outsiders who are in power.

However, there is a flip side to this as well. Repeatedly in communities of color, we've been told that the moderator must be sensitive and respectful of the target audience. Just because someone has a skin color or ethnicity similar to participants doesn't guarantee that he or she will be trusted and effective. Indeed, we've had disasters with academics from a racial category who weren't trusted by people within the community, or when we thought the key factor was race and later found that the moderator was seen as an outsider because he or she came from a different tribe, clan, or community.

The guiding principle that has been most helpful is to ask locals who should lead the discussion. In fact, this has been one of the most valuable tips in planning focus groups within different cultures, languages, races, and backgrounds. Every community and neighborhood has wise people who should be sought out when planning the study. These local people are well aware of the traditions, customs, and local circumstances that will make the study successful. Go to them and seek their wisdom. Don't stop with one. Go to several. Ask about the moderator, scheduling, incentives, and food, and also try out some of the questions. Don't expect that they will all agree, but listen for the reasons behind the advice.

Who can sanction the study? Without their approval, the study may not be feasible or practical. A task force or group of elders, influentials, or respected leaders might be invited to provide advice. Also, who can best offer advice on improving the study design, offer feedback on recruitment strategies, or assist in developing questions? These individuals may be different from the first group in that they are more similar to the target audience, more familiar with research protocol, or more familiar with the topic of the study. These individuals ensure that the focus group methodology is culturally sensitive and acceptable. Finally, who can assist with certain critical tasks in the focus group process, such as recruitment, moderating, or analysis and interpretation? The researcher might want to involve talented local individuals who are willing to receive instruction, offer their advice, and assist with these tasks.

Local residents can also help you find out about recent events or traditions that might influence the study. Occasionally, there are events that might change the plan, timing, audience, or questions of the study. In some communities, there can be long-standing issues relating to trust, respect, past experiences, and so on that are critical for the researcher to understand.

Ritual and tradition are important. When conducting focus groups, it is essential that researchers understand the culture and history. The researcher should consider when and where people talk, who is present during discussions, who is entitled to ask questions, and what protocol is used when asking questions.

Be attentive to foods. The food may take on special meaning and serve as a unifying factor or a trust-building experience. Listen to local advice when selecting foods.

Finally, remember that each person really only speaks for himself or herself in the focus group. No one person speaks on behalf of any group of people. Don't expect that one "leader" can tell you what is appropriate, offensive, tasteful, or wise. They speak from experiences and values, which may vary widely. Respectfully seek multiple viewpoints.

Focus Groups With International Groups and Organizations

By international groups, we are referring to groups conducted in developing countries that are sponsored by an international agency, a

TIP

Focus Groups With International Groups and Organizations

1. Avoid power differentials.
2. Consider cultural differences.
3. Use the local language.
4. Be less concerned about time.
5. Provide adequate confidentiality.
6. Provide benefit to participants.

research agency, or even an individual researcher. In these situations, there are often clear power differences between those sponsoring the research and those who are subjects of the research. This power differential plus cultural differences have the potential for communication problems.

Power differences almost always cause difficulties in focus group research. For a focus group to work, the participants must be willing to talk without feeling threatened.

Consider cultural differences that various people have when sharing insights on programs and products. In some environments, the cultural norm is to avoid criticism. Participants are not expected to identify problems or talk about solution strategies. Some individuals are exceedingly polite and diplomatic and talk only about the positive qualities. Or some participants assume that the purpose of the group is to find reasons to cut funding, so they are extremely positive.

Conduct the groups in the primary language of the participants. Avoid interpreters. This means that the moderator should be fluent in the language. If the moderator is not fluent, find someone who is and train him or her to lead the group. Have notes taken in the same language the moderator is using. Then translate the notes or audiotape back into English.

Think about who should moderate the group. Avoid moderators who occupy positions of power. Sometimes local residents are able to lead the group discussion, and in other situations, the international guest researcher is quite capable and nonthreatening.

Plan the study carefully so that you have listened to relevant agencies and groups that need to sanction the study. Also, listen to local wise people about timing, locations, and other factors relevant to the study.

Each culture has distinctive senses of time. The group may not begin at the designated time, and the two-hour time limit may be unimportant. The critical factor is the quality of the information that the researcher is obtaining.

Don't forget the importance of confidentiality. Participants may not necessarily trust the researchers, depending on what has happened in the past. Avoid group discussions on topics that can put individuals at risk after the researcher leaves the village or community.

Finally, consider how the study can be of benefit to the participants. Will study results be shared with participants? Will the study inform policy or future decisions?

SUMMARY

The focus group is able to produce meaningful information and do so in a manner that shows respect for traditions and uses language and culture differences as advantages. For focus groups to work, however, the researcher must be alert to certain modifications to the procedures. The researcher must be sensitive to establishing an environment where these individuals feel comfortable in talking. The researcher must approach each audience with respect, seeking their wisdom. When the researcher meets these expectations, the focus group yields impressive results.

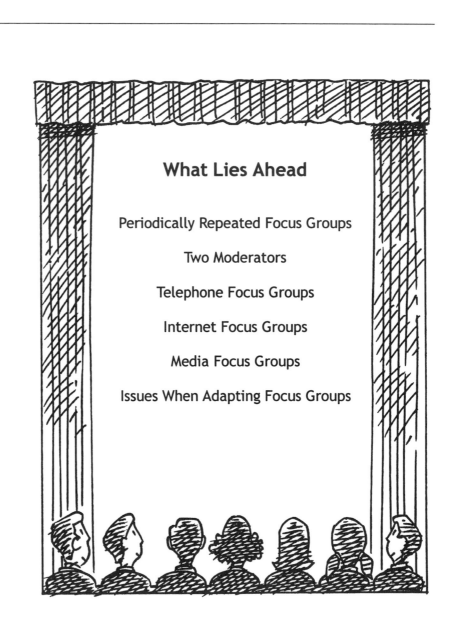

10

Modifications of Focus Groups

OK. So, we've been telling you there are certain procedures to follow when conducting a focus group study. We've been prescriptive. That's because we believe a researcher should understand and have practice using accepted procedures. Then, with wisdom that comes from experience, the researcher can adapt these procedures for different situations, considering the advantages and disadvantages of these adaptations. Modifications that have merit in certain situations include periodically repeated focus groups, focus groups with dual moderators, and telephone focus groups. Other modifications just shouldn't be called focus groups. This includes media focus groups.

Periodically Repeated Focus Groups

Periodically repeated focus groups can be done with the same participants or with different participants. Typically, the topic centers on a topic in which organizations need continuous feedback, such as, "How are we doing?" or "How can we improve customer satisfaction?" Some organizations invite different participants each time. For example, a community center might conduct quarterly focus groups with different people who use the facilities, or a state park system might conduct weekly focus groups with campers. In each of these situations, the organization is able to keep up with user perceptions and take corrective action as needed.

Repeated focus groups also can be conducted with the same participants with a time interval between sessions. This is helpful when the researcher wants to track changes in perceptions over time or to tap into opinions of a somewhat more informed group. For example, a museum brings in the same group of patrons each quarter and asks them for their perceptions. Participants in these groups become more sensitized to issues concerning the organization because they know they will be asked for their opinions. Over time, they become more like key informants than average customers.

Two Moderators

The structure of the focus group can be modified to accommodate two moderators. Moderators work together but represent different levels of expertise with focus groups and the topic of discussion. For example, one moderator may be an expert in conducting focus groups and a generalist on the topic of discussion, whereas the second moderator might know little about focus groups but be a specialist in the topic. In effect, this procedure allows for a subject matter expert in the focus groups but not in a manner that will unduly influence the group. Suppose that a community center wants to build a new recreational unit and decides to conduct a series of focus groups with members of the community. The moderator with expertise in focus groups might be complemented with a moderator with an architectural background who could present information on various alternative ideas suggested by the participants. This differs from the normal moderator and assistant moderator role because the second person regularly talks and presents information in the focus group, whereas normally, the assistant moderator is primarily a listener and note taker.

A variation of the use of complementary moderators is to have the sponsor of the focus group serve as the second moderator. This might include the director of the nonprofit agency or a member of the board of directors. These situations require caution because these individuals tend to be rather defensive and overreact when they hear negative comments. When they hear comments about things that are untrue, they want to make corrections. Furthermore, if this second moderator is an individual with local prominence or is in a respected position, the participants may be reluctant to provide candid feedback. If you decide to use this approach, be sure to select the person carefully and then carefully review expectations and remind him or her of appropriate and inappropriate behavior.

Telephone Focus Groups

Focus group discussions can be conducted on the telephone. With a conference call hookup, the moderator can carry on a focus group discussion with people scattered around the country. The telephone focus group offers the advantage of allowing participants to interact over distances at a fraction of the cost of transporting the same people to a central location.

The principal disadvantage of telephone focus groups is in the lack of nonverbal communication. Much is gained in focus groups by having people together and watching the participants—head nodding, signs of boredom, smiles, frowns, alertness, interest in the topic—all of which are unavailable on the telephone. A telephone focus group will lack the richness of in-person focus groups.

Telephone focus groups can be conducted with varying levels of sophistication. At one extreme, it can be conducted with limited resources and resemble a conference phone call. With more sophisticated telephone equipment, it is possible to have a console with lights and names to identify speakers, special switching devices that allow only one person to speak at a time, and lights that indicate when others are attempting to talk.

When we do telephone focus groups, we decrease the time, number of participants, and number of questions. Two hours is too long to be on the phone. We recommend one-hour telephone focus groups. Because we have less time, we recruit only four to six people for a phone focus group, and we limit the number of questions we ask. There is something else that we do for phone groups that we don't usually do for in-person groups—we send out the questions ahead of time. This seems to make the short time we have more productive. People know where we are going and know what they want to say and will stick with us mentally, even when we aren't together physically.

Again, we use telephone focus groups only when people would be difficult or impossible to physically get together.

Internet Focus Groups

Internet focus groups can be of several different types. On the simplest level, it is a chat line with questions posed by a leader or moderator and comments entered via the keyboard by participants at remote sites. On a more complicated level and with additional hardware and software, the communication can be by voice or even by voice and video. The greatest advantage is the low cost and the ability to link together people in far-flung locations. One major disadvantage is the use of keyboards for entering comments. Those with quick fingers and who are comfortable with written communications do quite well, expressing opinions rapidly and clearly. Those who have limited keyboard skills or problems with reading or writing will be at a major disadvantage. The Internet focus group is one step below the telephone focus group in the ability to get a sense of the group dynamics. Moderators who have used Internet groups have found that certain audiences seem to respond well to the process, such as young male computer experts. This type of group will continue to evolve with advancements in hardware and software.

The Internet focus group pushes the limits of what a focus group is. Is it really a focus group, or is it merely a chat line? The answer cannot be answered on superficial data. Internet groups become focus groups when the questions are focused, when participants can freely and openly communicate without inhibitions or fears, and when the moderator maintains control and moves the discussion in such a way to provide answers to the research question.

Media Focus Groups

The media have discovered the appeal of focus groups. Newspaper readers and television viewers like to read about or see others share opinions and ideas. These media groups have only a few common points with focus groups as described in this book. The argument for calling these sessions "focus groups" is that questions may be focused, participants may be preselected based on established criteria, and the moderator might be skillful in conducting the group, but these groups are about as far as possible from other characteristics that constitute focus groups—namely, a permissive, nonthreatening environment where confidentiality is ensured. These "media events" look like focus groups but aren't.

The purpose of these media sessions is to capture "sound bites" that are shared with the world. The individual has no assurance that comments will be used in context and no recourse if they are not. The participants are at the mercy of the media. These media focus groups typically have several methodological flaws that limit their value as serious research. First, they often consist of only one focus group. Furthermore, results from this one focus group are implicitly or explicitly generalized to a wider population. Second, the sessions are not conducted in a permissive, nonthreatening environment. Video and still cameras capture images throughout the session, constantly reminding participants of their potential for publicity. Recording devices capture everything said, but only a few comments will ever be published or aired. Third, the basis of selection is often to achieve a cross section of residents or voters, but many residents would self-select out of this public discussion. Only the most self-assured would submit to this type of group.

We encourage media to exercise caution and make a few adaptations. It would be more accurate if they called these sessions "group discussions," which would avoid some confusion to readers. If the media are serious about conducting focus groups and wish to call these sessions "focus groups," then they should consider a sequential series of discussions with varying levels of formality to determine the influence of cameras and recording equipment. For example, several groups might initially be conducted in the traditional focus group procedure without cameras, with homogeneous selection, and with explicit assurances of confidentiality. Then later, after the initial groups had been analyzed for themes, a second series of focus groups would allow cameras and seek public quotes. In this manner, the media could gain some sense of whether the participants modify their comments when they are "on record," taped, and photographed.

Media events called "focus groups" are entertainment—not research. We should place them in the same category as television or radio stations that conduct surveys using a pay-to-call vote. "Give us a call and vote on this important issue! Tell us your opinion! We want to hear from you!"

Issues When Adapting
Focus Groups

When adapting focus groups, the researcher should bear in mind what the focus group can do and what it can't do. Although there is elasticity in the procedure, too much stretch may snap the process. When adapting focus groups, consider the following:

- *The purpose.* It is appropriate to use focus groups to collect information, to listen, and to learn. Focus groups are not primarily intended to teach, to inform, or to have others sanction a decision.

- *Recruiting.* Focus group participants are preselected. Open invitations to the public or blanket invitations to a group are not used in focus group interviews.
- *The nature of the discussion.* A focused interview is composed primarily of open-ended questions that allow participants to select the manner of their response. It is not an open discussion of anything of interest.
- *The environment.* The focused interview is conducted in a permissive environment conducive to sharing, listening, and responding.

SUMMARY

Focus group interviews have been used successfully in a variety of situations. They can be conducted with the same people over a period of time, on the telephone, on the Internet, or with multiple moderators. All of these adaptations of focus group interviews possess the essential characteristics of focus groups. A limited number of homogeneous people are invited to participate in a focused discussion to provide data of a qualitative nature. The purpose is not to teach, to provide therapy, to resolve differences, or to achieve a consensus, but to obtain information in a systematic and verifiable manner. With that purpose in mind, the researcher should be encouraged to twist it a bit and discover just how robust and hardy focus group interviews really are. Media, on the other hand, may need to examine what they have called "focus groups" and either change the name (truth in advertising) to something like "group discussion" or make modifications to ensure that comments are not influenced by the media environment. For now, these media-based "focus groups" are best classified as entertainment—not research.

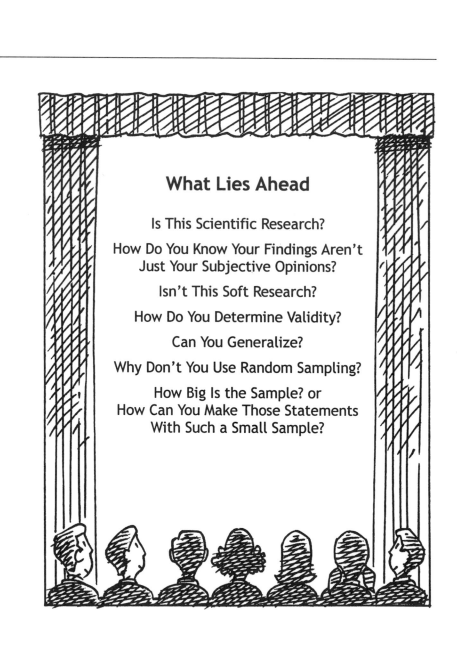

11

Answering Questions About the Quality of Focus Group Research

We want to talk about questions that are regularly asked about focus group research. Then we want to share options for answering these questions. You, as the field researcher, need to have workable answers to these questions. Not having answers gives the impression that you are unprepared, haven't thought about potentially critical topics, or don't have the qualifications needed for the task.

There are many ways to answer these questions. The ones we suggest are just a beginning—a jumping-off place. We encourage you to come up with even better answers.

You're going to get questions. Some questions will be about the topic, and other questions will be about your research methods. Questions will originate from colleagues, sponsors, interested individuals, focus group participants, and reviewers. A few questions will be vexing because they come at the time of reporting instead of at the time of planning, when they should have been addressed. During the oral report, you are intent on sharing the findings and placing emphasis on the results and recommendations, but instead, questions emerge about your methodology. The vexing questions aren't about results but about the research procedures and the philosophical underpinnings of the study. These questions can be hard to answer when they come unexpectedly. You've been concentrating on the results, and these process or philosophical questions catch you off guard. Here are some suggestions.

First, anticipate questions. By anticipating questions, you can think through answers to maximize clarity and conciseness. Anticipating questions begins with being thoughtful about your audience. What background have they had with this study and similar studies? Are they familiar with focus group studies? What is their degree of engagement or commitment to the study? What are their expectations of the report?

Think about the traditions of the organization and the environment of the report. One tradition is the hierarchical model in which the study has been "blessed and approved" by top management. Tough questions have already been asked in the planning stage, and the audience is now expected to applaud and cheer the results. We've seen this model fairly often within the corporate environment, and it is distinctly different from the academic environment. Still another is an environment whereby the audience is expected to take action based on the findings, and the questions that are asked are intended to help managers convey findings and action steps to subordinates. In this case, the questions asked of the reporter are the questions mid-managers anticipate being asked themselves. In effect, it is a train-the-trainer model on answering questions. Another environment is reporting at academic meetings and professional associations. These are some differences we've seen, but undoubtedly more exist. The circumstances should influence the way you answer questions. The degree of details and the manner of response will differ slightly in each environment.

Second, consider the reason for the question. Don't assume that the question necessarily reflects a desire for information. Ask yourself, Why is this question being asked? You'll never be completely certain of the reasons, but you will have a hunch that is based on past questions, on the context of the report, or on the person asking the question. We've seen several types of questioners:

- Some who ask questions truly want answers. They are curious and interested in what you are doing. They may have struggled themselves and are eager to learn new strategies and skills. These individuals may want more information about particular findings or the future uses of the study. *Response strategy:* Organize your response to achieve clarity and conciseness. Give the answer as best you can. If appropriate, ask the person for his or her thoughts.

- Some will ask questions, but they are really making statements. It may be a statement for or against your study, or it could be a statement on an entirely different topic. Don't assume that you need to have an answer. *Response strategy:* Thank the person for the comment and continue with other questions.

- Some ask questions to fill time, to get attention, or even in a desire to help you. *Response strategy:* Answer the question, invite someone else to answer, or postpone the answer for later.

- For some, the question is the beginning of the trap. The questioner is seeking to find fault or to expose a perceived inadequacy of the study. *Response strategy:* State or repeat the rationale for the study and why the methodology was deemed appropriate. Describe the systematic procedures. Clarify the limitations.

Sometimes questions reflect beliefs that someone holds about the nature of research and the scientific method. These beliefs are developed through reading and study, through the influence of people who tell us what is the proper and acceptable way of knowing, and through experience.

For some, research approaches are like religious beliefs. Religious groups hold a variety of views, and some contend that their group alone has the correct answers and approaches to life. Another view is that there is one preferred view among a number of other worthy beliefs. Still others will hold multiple views, not seeing any belief system as exclusive, holding to the view that one could hold different beliefs simultaneously. Our mantra is to be respectful and honoring of alternative views. We don't assume that we will be able to persuade people to abandon their beliefs. This is not the moment for conversion.

CAUTION

Answering a Different Question

A strategy, which we discourage, is answering a different question. This is regularly used in the political arena, especially in press conferences. Sometimes this is done inadvertently, such as when the question isn't understood and a rough attempt is made to provide an answer. Other times, the strategy is an overt attempt to switch the question to one that the respondent is able to answer. This strategy is not advised.

Let's begin by examining questions about focus group research methodology. At some point, you will be asked questions such as these, and your answers will need to be tailored to the specific situation. Besides the questions and our answers, we've also included some background information and thoughts about the question.

Q. Is This Scientific Research?

A. Scientific research takes several forms. In biological and physical science research, the intent is to discover cause and effect, to find relationships, to find predictability, or to discover laws of nature. In these forms of scientific research, control, replication, and proof through replication are crucial. There are several underlying assumptions. One is that the researcher has control over the environment. For example, the researcher can add more moisture or light and document the consequences on plants. Another assumption is that there are "laws of nature," and these laws are consistent, understandable, and predictable.

Social science research uses many of the same approaches but makes adaptations to fit the human experiences. Yes, focus group research is scientific research because it is a process of disciplined inquiry that is systematic and verifiable. It is not the type of scientific research that seeks to control and predict, but it is the type that seeks to provide understanding and insight.

Background

For decades, social scientists have sought to improve the quality of their research by perfecting scientific procedures. Social scientists adopted experimental design strategies used in physical and biological sciences. Randomization, control groups, and experimental designs became popular. However, scientists were soon disappointed, for although they learned a great deal, they found that this positivistic approach actually limited their thinking and overlooked valuable data. Consequently, other scientific procedures emerged that proved to be applicable to social science inquiry. A number of names were given to these scientific procedures, but in general, they belong to a category called qualitative research.

Thoughts

This question regularly comes from someone who has been told that there is only one right way to conduct scientific research, and that way is a positivistic method, whereby we set hypotheses, control the experiment, and then project to a population. We owe a great deal to the traditions of logical-positivistic scientific methods. Major discoveries can be attributed to this style of research and way of knowing. In fact, this way of thinking is so traditional and predominant within the United States that some people don't know there are other ways of knowing or of doing research.

Q. *How Do You Know Your Findings Aren't Just Your Subjective Opinions?*

A. We've approached this study, recognizing the importance of two guiding principles: researcher neutrality and systematic procedures. We've addressed researcher neutrality in several ways. The research team consisted of people with differing backgrounds to ensure that the results presented reflect multiple perspectives. Our research team was aware of the need for neutrality and the importance of capturing all participants' views.

Throughout the study, we've used accepted systematic procedures for data collection, data handling, and data analysis. We've used field notes and electronic recordings to capture the comments, which were then reviewed and used in the analysis process. During the focus group, we would ask participants to explain their views if we did not clearly understand what was said. Then, following the discussion, we offered a summary of key findings that participants verified. Our later debriefing and reports involved a team approach. We used accepted systematic steps in the analysis to identify key points and then compared results to other groups to identify patterns. For each point identified in our results, we have established a trail of evidence that can be verified. We have been very careful and are confident that the findings are an accurate reflection of what the focus group participants said. We are open to discussing alternate interpretations of the findings and recommendations.

Background

A study that is subjective is one in which researchers are so close and familiar with the study that their judgments influence the results.

Objectivity, on the other hand, makes use of instruments or standardized procedures that precisely measure something without human influence.

We use teams and standardized procedures to help us gather and analyze the data, so we aren't just paying attention to things that support our expectations or worldview, to things we like, or to things we understand. We are careful to distinguish the findings—what was said in the group—from our interpretations and recommendations. We expect more subjectivity in the interpretations and recommendations. But these are also the parts of the study that are open to debate. People with different backgrounds and different experiences may very well come up with different interpretations and recommendations.

Thoughts

It is hard to judge the intent of this question. Sometimes this is a friendly question where someone wishes to help the researcher. Other times, this is a cynical question inferring disrespect for certain types of research. Therefore, give thought as to how you answer. Be respectful and honoring of other points of view or research philosophies, even if others do not show respect for your views. Also, avoid becoming defensive as you give your answer. In general, we avoid words such as *subjective* versus *objective* or *soft* versus *hard*.

CHECKLIST

Answering Questions on Subjectivity (or Softness)

❑ Don't be surprised
❑ Be respectful
❑ Don't get defensive
❑ Assume they really want the answer
❑ Tell how people worked together to ensure neutrality
❑ Describe how data were captured
❑ Describe how data were verified
❑ Describe how data were analyzed

Now, do all the above in less than two minutes!

Q. *Isn't This Soft Research?*

A. If by *soft* you mean we haven't quantified people's reactions, then yes, you're right, we didn't quantify them. It wasn't our intent to quantify. Our intent was to find the range of feeling and opinion on this topic. We did that. If by *soft* you mean without standards or rigor, then no, it isn't soft. (Go on to explain processes.)

This study sought to obtain perceptions of people on a complex topic. No instrument is available to measure the multiple views of this changing and complex concept. Indeed, the only way to study it was to obtain the in-depth perceptions of participants. The results could not be expressed in numeric form but needed to take on a descriptive style.

Another way to answer this is to discuss the value of observing but not controlling the population. Our answer might look like this: "In positivistic research, the emphasis is placed on achieving control. Research is 'hard' if it uses sufficient controls that document what has happened. The environment is controlled, people are controlled in terms of what treatment they receive, and also the variables that affect the study are controlled. Many human environments, outside of the laboratory, cannot and should not be controlled. Our intent in this study was to observe, to listen, to document, and to report the perceptions of our target audience. Establishing controls would not have been appropriate."

Background

The words *soft* or *hard* are imprecise and misleading. *Hard* tends to refer to numbers, especially those coming from standardized sources of testing, measurement, surveys, or experimental design. On the other hand, *soft* typically refers to descriptive, observational, or interview data. Increasingly, scientists are avoiding these terms. The colloquial language of "hard research" and "soft research" is pejorative, simplistic, and sometimes inflammatory. These words imply a superior-subordinate relationship.

Q. *How Do You Determine Validity?*

A. We look at our procedures to determine whether we have used procedures that ensure that the results are trustworthy. Our research team was concerned about the quality of the information and that the results be an accurate reflection of how the participants felt and thought about the topic. We've taken several steps to ensure accuracy of the results.

We pilot tested the questions to ensure that they were understood. We listened to participants when designing the study to understand the conditions needed for free and open sharing. We used a team of moderators who were appropriate for the situation because of their training, experiences, background, and sensitivity. We listened carefully to participants, observed how they answered, and sought clarification on areas of ambiguity. Then, at the conclusion of each focus group, we asked participants to verify our summary comments. We used systematic analysis procedures. In summary, we've followed accepted protocol to ensure that results are trustworthy and accurate.

Background

Essentially this is a question about trusting or judging the results. In the positivistic tradition, it has been important to determine validity because a test or instrument was created to measure something, and occasionally, it would measure the wrong thing. In these quantitative studies, the instrument was a proxy for what was really measured. By contrast, in focus group research, there are no proxies. Words of the participant are used to find out participants' feelings, thoughts, or observations about the topic of discussion. The researcher is able to draw on multiple sources of information that are not normally available to the quantitative researcher. The focus group researcher observes the answers and has an opportunity to follow up and probe to

amplify or clarify the response. Moreover, the focus group researcher can feed back the key points and seek verification from participants.

Thoughts

We are coming to the conclusion that validity is overemphasized in qualitative research. Instead, one should concentrate on good practice.

The goal of the researcher is to understand the respondents' points of view and to be able to communicate these to the audience. For this to occur, a researcher must be concerned with conducting quality studies. Good practices are described in Chapters 2 through 7 and include planning, asking questions, moderating, finding participants, analyzing, and reporting. These actions aren't meant to be lockstep, cookie-cutter procedures but rather guiding principles that inform researcher behavior. They must be modified and adjusted as the environment and situation warrant.

In summary, we suggest that the researcher worry less about the traditional concerns of validity and instead be ready to answer the following question: What are you doing to ensure that you have followed the steps associated with quality research?

Q. *Can You Generalize?*

A. This study is not intended to generalize. Our goal is to go in-depth into a topic, and therefore, we spend a sizable amount of time conducting research with a small number of people. Other research methods, by contrast, do not go "in-depth" but use closed-ended questions with limited response choices that offer breadth instead of depth. The studies that offer breadth are the ones used to make generalizations.

So from a strict sense, one cannot generalize, but what we suggest is the concept of transferability. That is, when a person wants to use the results, he or she should think about whether the findings can transfer into another environment. What we suggest is that you consider the methods, procedures, and audience and then decide the degree to which these results fit the situation you face.

Background

Transferability, according to Lincoln and Guba (1989), is parallel to the positivistic concept of generalizability, except that it is the receiver (not the sender or researcher) who decides if the results can be applied

BACKGROUND

For more information, see the following:

Lincoln, Y., & Guba, E. (1989). *Fourth generation evaluation.* Newbury Park, CA: Sage. See especially Chapter 8, "Judging the Quality of Fourth Generation Evaluation."

to the next situation. The person reviewing the research looks over the conditions, situations, and procedures and then decides the degree of fit to the second situation.

Thoughts

Expect a question about generalizability when presenting focus group results. Generalizability is a nifty concept. Through randomization and adequate sampling, a researcher is able to promise generalizability. With generalizability, the researcher describes the degree to which these results are expected to occur in other places. By contrast, focus group research involves only a limited number of people who may not be selected in a random manner. Therefore, don't promise generalizability. Instead, suggest that those who seek to use the results look over the study; examine the procedures, methods, and the analysis strategies; and then decide the degree to which this might be applied to their situation. What may be transferred are the larger theoretical concepts as opposed to the specific findings.

Q. Why Don't You Use Random Sampling?

A. Because random sampling isn't appropriate. In focus group research, the strategy is to use purposeful sampling whereby the researcher selects participants based on the purpose of the study. For example, the research might be to study users of a program, teenagers in the community who have experienced violence, or diabetic men older than age 50. In each situation, we are seeking these kinds of people because they have special knowledge or experiences that are helpful in the study. They are what Michael Patton (1990) calls "information-rich" cases. Focus groups are composed of homogeneous groups of people—people with something in common that is relevant to the topic of study. Random sampling of the population would be a waste of time and resources. However, the researcher often assembles a pool of potential participants and then randomly selects from within this pool of qualified individuals. This level of randomization is regularly done, and it helps minimize selection bias.

Thoughts

In quantitative research, considerable attention is placed on random sampling. The reason is that randomization helps ensure that a sample is a snapshot of the larger population. The size and the randomness determine the quality of the sample. If the size is small and the sample not random, it will be suspect. Therefore, it is no surprise that quantitative researchers are concerned about the size and randomness in focus group studies.

BACKGROUND

References to Consider

Be able to give the logic as cited by experts. Consider looking over the following:

Glaser, B., & Strauss, A. (1967). *The discovery of grounded theory.* Chicago: Aldine. Note discussions of theoretical sampling.

Patton, M. Q. (1990). *Qualitative evaluation and research methods.* Newbury Park, CA: Sage. Read Chapter 5 on "Designing Qualitative Studies."

Strauss, A., & Corbin, J. (1990). *Basics of qualitative research: Grounded theory and procedures and techniques.* Newbury Park, CA: Sage. Review Chapter 11 on "Theoretical Sampling."

Q. How Big Is the Sample? or, How Can You Make Those Statements With Such a Small Sample?

A. In this form of research, the quality of the study is not dependent on the size of the sample. The intent is to achieve theoretical saturation, which is akin to redundancy. We are watching for patterns in our interview results, and we will sample until we discover that we have "saturated" the theory or found redundant information. In focus group research, the rule of thumb has been to conduct three or four focus groups with a particular audience and then decide if additional groups (or cases) should be added to the study. Large-scale studies with divergent populations often require more groups, but our goal is to determine the variability of a concept or idea.

Background

Patton (1990) offers an example that might be helpful in your answer:

> Piaget contributed a major breakthrough to our understanding of how children think by observing his own two children at length and in great depth. Freud established the field of psychoanalysis based on fewer than ten client cases. Bandler and Grinder founded neurolinguistic programming by studying three renowned and highly effective therapists. . . . Peters and Waterman formulated their widely followed eight principles for organizational excellence by studying 62 companies, a very small sample of the thousands of companies one might study.
>
> The validity, meaningfulness, and insights generated from qualitative inquiry have more to do with the information-richness of the cases selected and the observational/analytical capabilities of the researcher than with sample size. (p. 185)

Thoughts

Small sample size will be hard for some researchers to swallow. Quantitative research procedures have repeatedly called for randomization and adequate sample size. Indeed, sample size is an indicator of quality in quantitative research. The logic of sampling in qualitative research is different. The purpose of the study and the nature of what is discovered determine the sample type and size.

References

Belisle, P. (1998). Digital recording of qualitative interviews. *Quirk's Marketing Research Review, 12*(11), 18, 60-61.

Bellenger, D. N., Bernhardt, K. L., & Goldstrucker, J. L. (1976). Qualitative research techniques: Focus group interviews. In T. J. Hayes & C. B. Tathum (Eds.), *Qualitative research in marketing* (pp. 10-25). Chicago: American Marketing Association. (Also reprinted in *Focus group interviews: A reader,* by J. B. Higginbotham & K. K. Cox, Eds., 1979, Chicago: American Marketing Association)

Debus, M. (1990). *Handbook for excellence in focus group research.* Washington, DC: Academy for Educational Development.

Glaser, B., & Strauss, A. (1967). *The discovery of grounded theory.* Chicago: Aldine.

Goldman, A. E., & McDonald, S. S. (1987). *The group depth interview.* Englewood Cliffs, NJ: Prentice Hall.

Greenbaum, T. L. (1998). *The handbook for focus group research.* Thousand Oaks, CA: Sage.

Jourard, S. M. (1964). *The transparent self.* Princeton, NJ: Van Nostrand.

Kelleher, J. (1982). Find out what your customers really want. *Inc, 4*(1), 88, 91.

Kornfield, J. (1993). *A path with heart.* New York: Bantam.

Krueger, R. A., & King, J. A. (1998). *Involving community members in focus groups.* Thousand Oaks, CA: Sage.

Lazarfeld, P. (1986). *The art of asking why.* New York: Advertising Research Foundation. (Original work published in 1934 in *The National Marketing Review*)

Lincoln, Y., & Guba, E. (1989). *Fourth generation evaluation.* Newbury Park, CA: Sage.

Merton, R. K., Fiske, M., & Kendall, P. L. (1956). *The focused interview.* Glencoe, IL: Free Press.

Money not the only motivation for respondents. (1991, May 27). *Marketing News, 25,* 11, 17.

Morgan, D. L. (1997). *Focus groups as qualitative research.* Thousand Oaks, CA: Sage.

Morgan, D. L., & Krueger, R. A. (Eds.). (1998). *The focus group kit.* Thousand Oaks, CA: Sage.

Patton, M. Q. (1990). *Qualitative evaluation and research methods.* Newbury Park, CA: Sage.

Rice, S. A. (Ed.). (1931). *Methods in social science.* Chicago: University of Chicago Press.

Roethlisberger, F. J., & Dickson, W. J. (1938). *Management and the worker.* Cambridge, MA: Harvard University Press.

Rogers, C. R. (1942). *Counseling and psychotherapy.* New York: Houghton Mifflin.

Schmit, J. (1993, June 1). Deep secrets told among passengers. *USA Today,* pp. 1B-2B.

Strauss, A. (1988). *Qualitative analysis for social scientists.* New York: Cambridge University Press.

Strauss, A., & Corbin, J. (1990). *Basics of qualitative research: Grounded theory and procedures and techniques.* Newbury Park, CA: Sage.

Vaughn, S., Schummn, J. S., & Sinagub, J. (1996). *Focus group interviews in education and psychology.* Thousand Oaks, CA: Sage.

Yin, R. K. (1984). *Case study research.* Beverly Hills, CA: Sage.

Index

About the Authors

Richard A. Krueger, Ph.D., is a professor and evaluation leader for the University of Minnesota. He teaches qualitative research methods and program evaluation, as well as serving as the evaluation leader for the University of Minnesota Extension Service. Although trained as a quantitative researcher, he was drawn to qualitative research. He has spent the past twenty years learning about, practicing, and teaching focus group interviewing.

Mary Anne Casey, Ph.D., is a consultant to government agencies and nonprofit organizations. She helps them design and conduct individual and group interviews as a way of listening to their employees and customers. The information is typically used to plan and evaluate programs. She has previously worked for the Kellogg Foundation, the University of Minnesota, and the State of Minnesota.

Dick and Mary Anne teach workshops on how to conduct focus groups and often work together on focus group studies. Besides sharing an interest in focus groups, Mary Anne and Dick share a home life. They are married and live in St. Paul, Minnesota, with two cats—Kitty O'Shea and Maud Gonne. Dick also practices the art of motorcycle admiration (standing in the garage looking at his Harley), and Mary Anne reads about, dreams about, and enjoys working in gardens.

DATE DUE

MR 20 '03			
AP 26 '04			

DEMCO 38-297